Dear Catherine,

Thankyou so much for your support!

Conducting Chaos

A Guide to Teaching Improv to Kids and Teens

♥ Jessica Arjet

Jessica Arjet

ISBN: 978-1-950186-26-6

Cover illustration by CB Creates
Instagram @cbcreates2020

Cover and interior design by Jennifer Leigh Selig
www.jenniferleighselig.com

MANDORLA BOOKS
WWW.MANDORLABOOKS.COM

DEDICATION

To my two children Catherine and Henry - my first students
and my loving partner Andreas Fabis - my best supporter

TABLE OF CONTENTS

INTRODUCTION

In 2006, I had just graduated from three levels of improv at the Hideout Theatre in Austin, Texas. I was thrilled with all I had learned and with how improv had fundamentally shifted some of my personal paradigms and improved my life. I had learned about and begun to embrace being positive, accepting risk, and being in the moment. I had grown up in theater as a child and loved the stage, but there was something different and magical and dare I say—life-changing about improv.

At the time I was homeschooling my 11-year-old daughter, which involved us hanging out with lots of other kids around the same age. I started teaching them a game or two I'd learned in class and they really seemed to like it.

Based on that, I rented some space and began teaching an improv class for kids. I had been a drama teacher on and off for years, so this was a natural role for me. I advertised to the homeschool community and held the classes on Tuesday afternoons. I was grateful that the kids in my homeschool group all signed up, in addition to a few more kids I didn't know.

The kids loved it and seemed to be really embracing the same concepts that I had found to be so life-changing. They seemed relieved to have a place where risk was expected and failure was a sign of playing hard. I could see the simple exercises helping them find the power of creativity. They gained in confidence and became more socially adept. It was a great class.

Even more students signed up for the second round of classes, and all the kids developed even more. I found that I LOVED teaching these kids and watching them struggle with—and eventually embrace—these beautiful concepts.

However, by this time I had taught them all the games I knew. At the end of the class run, I sat the kids down and said that I wouldn't teach the class again, because I didn't have anything to teach them. They all just stared at me with wide eyes.

"I don't know anything else, guys," I explained. By this time the eyes had started to look sad, and I began to panic.

I tried to explain. "If I taught another class, I'd just be figuring it out as we went along."

"Okay, cool," the kids said.

And that's how I began developing an improv program for kids.

Over the years I've seen dozens of kids grow and change through improv.

One child refused to even walk onstage and just watched the other kids play for the entire first semester. For the showcase, he sat with his parents and wouldn't come near the stage. In the second semester, he tried the games and played briefly in the final showcase. In the third semester, he bounded into class and took over the stage. His parents were literally in tears when they saw his final performance. He is now a concert pianist and his parents credit improv with his ability to play in front of other people.

Another child was going through a rough gender identity exploration. Playing the different characters and stories let them play with their identity in a low-stress setting. They said that, other than home, improv class was the only place they felt safe and they could be themself, no matter what self was present that day.

Two of our special-needs teens found their first friend ever in improv class.

And of course, I've seen children grow and change in a more typical way, turning from gangly kids to poised and confident adults.

Probably my favorite comment was from a child I taught for six years: "Thanks to Miss Jessica, I'm a much less awkward teen than I would have been otherwise."

Here's what I've learned: improv helps kids through the difficult process of growing up. It supports them in exploring different voices and identities in a safe and fun environment. It teaches them how to work and create with others. It introduces a comfortability with risk so that when they make mistakes, they can move on from them. And it creates a positive environment where students can use performance and creativity to process their complex and ever-changing lives.

I firmly believe that every child in the world should have at least a little experience with improv. That's why I'm writing this book.

Also, improv classes make money! I always joke that the Hideout Theatre's second-quarter profits are all thanks to me and summer camp. (Not only do I work there, but now I'm one of the owners.) Summer camp and youth classes may not make all of our profit, but they do make working in the arts a bit more sustainable.

Ultimately, though, the best reason to teach improv to kids is because it's so much fun. What other job requires you to play silly games and laugh until your sides hurt while experiencing the joy of teaching your passion to the next generation? Improv is fun to learn, and even more fantastic to teach.

CHAPTER ONE

GET READY! WHAT YOU NEED TO KNOW

Once I decided that I was going to really teach improv, I thought I had it all figured out. I walked into that next improv class with a list of games to teach. After a few weeks one kid asked me, "Why? Why did we do this game? Why are we learning this?"

"Ummm ... because it's fun?" I answered. It wasn't exactly a wrong answer, but it left out a lot and made me realize that knowing a few games wasn't enough.

To be a good improv teacher, you should not just know games, but understand the underlying philosophy of what those games are teaching and why.

You should also have an understanding of kids—their basic needs, their developmental stages, and how to handle them in a group setting.

Know Improv

If you haven't taken any improv classes yourself, then you really should. I'd suggest at least three levels of improv to help you understand the basics. But even a weeklong intensive would be super helpful.

I personally love taking classes from all sorts of teachers. I not only enjoy the content of the different classes, but I adore watching the way different teachers teach. When you see another teacher at their craft, you pick up some valuable lessons beyond what they're teaching. You see the way they start a class, how they get the attention of the class, how much they share of themselves, how they correct people; you get a window into how another person gives the information they know to others. This can be invaluable for you in developing your own teaching style.

I often warn my teens that I've taken a new workshop so they know they'll have to put up with me trying to teach the games I've learned. They roll their eyes and groan, but they love learning the new things I bring back. We'll work together to tweak things and figure out the way they work best for us as a class.

If you're just getting started with teaching, make sure you know the WHY of the basic improv principles. Really dig deep into why you need to be comfortable with risk. Have a nuanced understanding of why we say "yes, and!" I hear kids new to our program tell me the rule is "never say no," and I just cringe, because someone who didn't know their improv principles well taught them that.

Know Kids

Working with kids is really different from working with adults. I've worked with kids for most of my life, so teaching them came pretty naturally to me—but then when I taught my first class with adults I was flummoxed!

When you're talking to adults, they will just listen and sometimes nod their heads. They don't run around when I get too long-winded; they check out, but you can't tell because their expressions don't change. If they don't understand something, they don't look confused or ask, they just struggle on. I was always unsure if they were getting me or not. On the other hand, you can let them go to the bathroom by themselves. That's certainly an advantage!

Kids are not just shorter than adults—they have significantly different needs, and their needs change at different ages. I'll cover this pretty extensively in Chapter 7.

If you've never taught kids or teens before, you'll want to get a little experience under your belt. The best way to do this is to offer to help someone who already works with the age group you intend to work with.

Find someone who's already a teacher in any subject and tag along with them. That's the best way to learn, but any way you can find to be around your intended age group will be good. Volunteer to help out with a science fair, or in a religious school class, or with a child's sports team. Volunteer in the classroom or at school events or any extracurricular activities. This will give you a little more comfort with kids and will let you watch the main teacher/coach/facilitator in action so you can pick up some tips from them as well. Remember: steal all the good ideas you can!

Know Games

I have a plethora of game lists written in notebooks, phone lists, and on the backs of envelopes. I collect games like other people collect stamps—I always want more! Because, believe it or not, no matter how many games you write down on your list, sooner or later you'll run out of them. You'll be standing there saying, "Next we're going to … ah … um …" and then one of your kids will shout "Category Die!" and you'll have to play **Category Die** … again … for the fifth time that day.

There are some fabulous resources out there to help you avert this disaster. *The Playbook: Improv Games for Performers* by William Hall is the gold standard of improv game books. But a simple Google search will yield up enough games to keep you safe from **Category Die** for semesters! When I mention a game in this book, it will be in bold, and you'll find it described in the index at the back of this book.

Know Improv Philosophy

I would hope that everyone teaching improv has had at least a few classes and hopefully some time on stage, but these aren't enough. If your understanding of improv philosophy is as shaky as mine was in the beginning, then read up on improv to solidify your understanding. Some of my favorite books on the subject are *Improv for Storytellers* by Keith Johnstone, *improvise: Scene From the Inside Out* by Mick Napier, and *Acting On Impulse: The Art of Making Improv Theater* by Carol Hazenfield. These will help you understand why you're doing the games you're doing and how to correct them if and when they go astray.

Also, it will help you say really smart things when your kids ask you, "Why?"

CHAPTER TWO

GET SET! CREATING A CLASSY CURRICULUM

Now that you've got your improv experience, your kid experience, a list of games, and a pretty good understanding of the principles of improv, your first step in actually teaching real children is to decide on your underlying philosophy or goal.

Of course, you can teach classes without an underlying goal, and it'll be fine. I did that for at least a year, and it was fine. But only fine. The point of this book is to make you a great teacher and your classes great classes. Fine is just not good enough—kids deserve better than fine.

After those first couple of classes, I started realizing that I did have a philosophy, even if I hadn't stated it. Sitting down and really puzzling it out, I came up with this mission statement for my program: "The Hideout Theatre uses improv as a powerful and delightful tool to help children develop and grow both as people and as performers."

You're welcome to steal this and use it as your own. But maybe you want something slightly different. Maybe your goals are not the same as mine. In that case you'll need to come up with your own philosophy.

Here are some suggestions.

First, try to envision the kids you'll be working with, or if you already teach, really think about the kids in your class. Imagine them in your mind—their silly faces, their foibles and their strengths. What do you want for these kids? How do you want to impact them as a teacher? What do you want them to have gained after a class with you?

Maybe what you want is a safe place for kids to be wacky and have fun. Awesome!

Maybe you want to develop really fine improv performers who will blow an audience away. Great!

Maybe you're like me and see improv as a tool to help these silly little monkeys grow into the truest and best versions of themselves. Fantastic!

Whatever you land on as your philosophy and your goals is great, and will help you figure out how to approach the subject AND your overall program. Marketing and talking to parents is so much easier when you can articulate why you're doing this and what the kids will get from your classes.

Your Curriculum

Once you know what you want to teach, developing a curriculum becomes much easier. The kids will constantly be asking, begging, cajoling you to play their favorite games. If you know what you're teaching and why, it's then easier to keep on track and play the games that will help them develop their skills. The curriculum is the blueprint for you and other teachers to follow, so you can do more than just play **Alien Translator** for an hour straight. Believe me, that gets old!

The Hideout Curriculum

On my website, I offer my Hideout curriculum for download. However, I suggest that you don't just take this and use it unchanged. You'll need to teach to your strengths and to the needs of your program and your goals for your kids. In fact, when I give this curriculum to my teachers, I always let them know that they'll need to be able to be flexible and able to change in the moment. Let's be real—if the kids are bouncing off the walls, then quiet sitting-down work is what you need, and it doesn't really matter what the curriculum says.

What follows is the process of developing your own curriculum.

The Format of a Curriculum

Because I have an extensive encyclopedia of improv games in my head, I generally can categorize them according to what purpose they serve, what particular specific challenges they afford, and how they illustrate overall concepts and address problem areas.

However, when I need to pull up the next game in class, I tend to go blank. The kids are excited, or frustrated, or loud, or asking me questions and, despite all my years of experience with both kids AND improv, I literally cannot come up with the next appropriate game when a child is climbing me like a monkey climbs a tree. This is why I have a regular lesson plan.

For each day, or lesson, you'll want to make sure there is a list of exercises that are clear and easy to understand. In addition, you'll want to make sure there are notes about why you're doing this, or any extra comments that will make the running of this exercise easier or more successful. This preparation comes with an extra bonus: if your program becomes so successful and you need to train new teachers to help you carry the load, you'll have this paper trail you can share which will make them more successful in presenting your material.

Even if you're the only teacher, having a regular list of exercises with notes will help you to follow your own plan and make sure you have a really coherent set of lessons. That way you'll spend more time as a teacher and less time as a monkey tree.

Developing the Components

Once you have your mission statement in place, then you can start breaking that mission down into smaller pieces that we could call goals. And you'll need to figure out what the underlying skills are that you need to fulfill your mission and your ultimate goals.

At the Hideout, our goal is first to have a fun environment in which our kids can explore and grow as little humans. Our second goal is to create performers who will make exciting shows for audiences. And finally, our third goal is to enhance the overall experience of childhood for our kids, providing a platform for them to make friends while having loads of fun.

Once we know our overall mission and goals, we can turn those into program components. At the Hideout, these are the components of our program, in order of importance.

> **Fun** — Fun is why we're doing this in the first place. Having fun makes it easier to learn and grow. We use fun—enjoyment, excitement, delight—as a guide to showing us what to lean into and what to let go.

Embracing Failure — Being able to fail and move on is very important in life and in improv. If a person can fail happily, then they can take any "mistake" and turn it into a gift or opportunity. Every improvisor fails—the difference between the great players and the weaker players is that the great players either play off their failures or just move on to the next thing, whereas the weaker players either freak out and start doing whatever will make them feel safe, or blindly stick to something that's not working. We want our kids to be great at failing!

Saying Yes, And — When a person works with others, they need to accept their ideas so that the scene or game can flow. Not just accept them, but add to them, develop them. In improv, we bring our own creativity, and, together with our scene partner, we build scenes that are a magic amalgamation of all the creativity in the room. We teach kids to accept the offers of others and add to them enthusiastically.

Being Obvious — In improv, being obvious allows us to say what is actually there, to recognize what's happening and call it out, hopefully to hilarious effect. We teach our kids that stating what's obvious keeps them connected to the audience and their scene partner, and ultimately allows their own brilliant creativity to shine through.

Taking Care of Each Other — We emphasize with our kiddos that idea of working creatively with other people—their ideas, their offers, and their characters—requires taking them into consideration and taking care of the group as well as themselves. This step makes the "yes, and" work. Yes to self, and yes to others. We're all in this together.

Developing Characters — Exploring characters helps our kids discover different aspects of themselves and play with who they're and how they present themselves to the word. Different, fully-developed characters make scene work much more interesting and engaging.

Developing Stories — Stories help our kids contextualize their own lives and look at themselves as actors in the stories they're co-creating. We teach our kids that storying their scenes and shows makes them much more engaging. Stories help to provide a framework on which to hang all the rest of the work of improv.

Developing Space Work/Stage Picture — We teach our kids about the concept of "space work"—how knowing how to use the space on the stage allows their scenes be much more dynamic and interesting. Showing their emotions through what they're doing will build a rich layer to the scenes.

Each of these major components can be the focus of a single class in the series, or the focus of several classes. This is the backbone of knowing what to teach when.

Obviously, what you'll want to teach will vary. You might add in components or take out ones that seem less important. That is all good. You'll want to have a curriculum that's unique to your program and your goals and your kids. Once you have some basic tenets established, you can start breaking them down into lesson-sized pieces that will work with your timeline.

In this process you'll want to look at what components you need to put in place first in order to develop other components. For example, you may discover you need to tackle embracing failure before you look at developing characters because you want to make sure your kids are okay with taking the risks they'll need to take in order to develop those interesting characters. Otherwise, they may come up with great characters and then they'll say, "I don't know why I did that. It's dumb."

Building the Lessons

After you have your focus for each class period, it's time to think about how to teach that to the kids. This is a typical class structure:

Name/bonding games
Warm-ups
Exercises to teach the daily class focus
Performance games that highlight the skill for that week

With your focus in mind, ask yourself, what bonding games would support the class' focus? Keep your actual kids in mind when you're considering this—not the kids you had last year or the year before but these kids you have with you now—what can you do at their level to create an environment where they have to rely on and work with the other kids in class toward your goal for them? If you present a game and there is a lot of giggling, you'll know you're on the right track!

What warm-up games will get them ready for the exercises that are coming? Warm-ups should be pretty easy to play and master. If they're successful here, then it's easier for them to do the exercises which might be a bit more challenging. Here your goal is a room full of kids who feel confident and excited about what's coming next. Look for open body language, laughter, and comfortable chatter to show you that they're ready for the exercises.

Next look at the exercises. What exercises will teach and support the focus for the class? Of course these should also be fun, but it's okay here if the kids have to start thinking a bit. Come up with exercises and games that will stretch them and make them have to lean in to figure it out. That is less pure fun, and more challenging, but ultimately the kids become very satisfied when they're able to master these exercises. Look for concentration, flashes of inspiration, and kids jumping up to play as an indication that you're on the right track.

Finally, take a look at the performance games. What performance games will support the current lesson and will help them deepen their understanding of what's going on this week? Performance games are where you combine the challenge and the fun while you work the concepts that you're teaching this week. In a way, the performance part of class is your students' reward for doing well earlier. This is the sweet dessert to the mighty meal of improv exercises.

While you're building your lessons, keep in mind that smaller is better. Some improv concepts are big, so it's great to break them into their smallest possible component. For example, if you're teaching yes and, you want to start with the concept of accepting. A warm-up like **Sound Ball**, where you have to repeat the sound that another person made, is a great one for starting this process. In **Sound Ball**, you have the simplest form of acceptance, since you just repeat what the other person did. Once your kids are able to simply accept, then you can build in more complexity.

Through it all, you'll always want to watch the energy of your class. If you have a lot of high focus, mostly verbal games, you'll want to throw in an energy game to make sure they have a break and a bit of physical refreshment. Conversely, if you're playing a lot of high energy games and the kids start getting too hyper and unfocused, a slower-paced brain game can be a good way to bring them back under control so they can keep learning.

Name games (Shootout, Adjective Circle, Zombie Tag) are good ways of helping you and the kids remember the names of the other kiddos. Names are important to kids. They're a concrete part of their identity, and when most kids don't have a strong sense of who they're yet, saying and enforcing their names over and over again can give them a feeling of safety at the beginning of class, especially if they're somewhat shy or nervous.

Eye contact (Pass the Clap, You, Zip-Zap-Zop) is an essential part of good improv, as well as an essential part of good social skills. It's very important to work on this right at the top because this will encourage bonding in a very safe and non-threatening way. Good eye contact forces kids to be open to one another on a more emotional level and will make the class a little quicker to accept each other. At the same time, this will show the kids how important non-verbal communication is. They will quickly learn they can communicate a lot just by looking someone else in the eye.

Simultaneous games (Pass the Clap, Evolution, Protest Signs), when kids are doing things at the same time or chanting together, create a cohesion in the class. When kids are doing things together, it supports the value of working together, which is a necessary foundation for improv. And it's often a stretch for kids—in my experience, working together does not come easy until they're closer to the tween ages of 10-13. But these simultaneous games are easily accomplished and there is a huge amount of satisfaction in all of us humans when we're able to tune in and be a part of something larger than ourselves. If your kids can get on the same page and chant together, then you know that bonding is well underway.

Touching (Untie the Knot, Blind Trust Walks, People to People) is part of our fundamental nature as primates. We gain a lot of information from others and about others by touching. And kids are no exception—they need touch socially and as a source of communication.

You have to be careful with touching, however, and state some boundaries up front. For instance, you'll need to tell the kids not to touch any body part that would be covered by a bathing suit. Some kids LOVE touching each other in any way possible. Other kids are shyer and you'll have to make sure they're protected from the exuberance of the touchers. The touchers will get so excited that they will often end up falling on top of each other and maybe even hurting other kids. So it will be important to set strong boundaries in this area to keep everyone safe, both psychologically and physically.

Warm-ups

Once you've got the kids working together, then it will be time to warm them up. Many of the above exercises will also double as warm-ups. They don't need to be done in order, and you don't have to do each every day. It's best if you assess what the kiddos need during the first five or so minutes of class, then use the appropriate warm-ups to make sure they're ready to roll.

Body — you can literally just have them stretch. I have a series of stretches that go from top to toe. One of my teachers does something more strenuous, something she calls "Monster Yoga." What you do doesn't matter as much as making sure the body is engaged and ready to move in a coordinated fashion. This allows the kids to get their wiggles out. It also gets them moving in unity with you and the rest of the class. And when the body wakes up, it's easier for the kids to be present with themselves in the space.

Brain (Convergence, Word Association, One Frog) — Any exercises or games that make the kids run through mental gymnastics are good. These get the kids focused and ready to let the creative part of their brains take over and work hard. Verbal kids love these types of games, and since that kind of kid is often not as skilled at the traditional large motor playground games, it's fun for them to have a space where they can play successfully in groups with other kiddos.

Energy (Bunny Bunny, Cat and Mouse, House-Creature-Flood, Zombie Tag) — It may seem weird, but kids do also need energy warm-ups. If they're tired or not ready to play, they often show this by being jumpy and anxious. A few high energy warm-ups are perfect for getting them back in sync.

Story Warm-ups (Story Spine, Three-Headed Expert) — You'll want to save these warm-ups for after you've introduced your lesson on story. Kids inherently love telling stories, and it's nice to have some low stakes warm-ups where they can be as silly as they like. These are lower energy games, so make sure you're intentional about using these either before or after your energy warms ups.

Exercises

As I said above, you'll want to come into each session knowing your teaching priorities. Are you teaching yes, and? Are you teaching being obvious? Are you teaching commitment? Once you know what you want to teach, then you figure out which games will create the conditions for the kids to discover these principles and hone them through fun practice.

When you begin to teach an exercise, I've mentioned that it's best to break it down into the smallest possible component and do that first, then slowly up the challenge level until your kids are playing it at the level you want them to. After that, and this may sound counter-intuitive but hear me out, you'll want to playfully push the game too hard, make it too difficult so that they end up breaking it or the game falls apart. That way they will experience the full gamut of the possibilities of the game—some easy success, some challenge, and some failure, but failure in a way that's playful and fun and shows that failure is a potential or even probable outcome of pushing yourself hard. You want them to understand that failure is simply a boundary to work with and not an end point to quit at.

The kids should be smiling and laughing through this process of failure (I know, I warned you it was counter-intuitive!)—if they start to frown or get anxious and tight, then they're probably not learning and are just afraid of getting it wrong. Kids spend a lot of time being wrong—their entire focus in life is figuring out how to get this life thing correct enough so they can enjoy it! So, having a hard time with a game can be really frustrating for some kiddos. If you think they just need to work through it then you can continue, but if it goes for too long, you'll want to back down and go back to the easier components again. Or find a way to make it more playful again. If the child can go from being anxious and worried about the game to finding the fun in it again—that in itself is a great lesson.

It's also totally okay to bail on a game at times. Just make sure to take the heat on yourself rather than the kids. Let them know it's not their fault they couldn't learn the game, that you must have just explained it wrong. I take several failure bows during class, and this is one of the best places for a big bow! Plus, you're modeling important lessons about accepting and moving past failure for them.

A few well-placed questions after the exercise can make a ton of difference. "When you agreed to everything she said, how did that change the scene?" "Why do you think it worked so much better that time?" "What happens when you have to say the first thing and you don't have time to think?" It's much better to let the kids discover good improv lessons than to tell them what they need to do. A good question can help them find and articulate the lesson until it settles into their bodies and minds in a way that telling them the lesson just doesn't replicate. If you've gone through a few exercises and they're still having a hard time, try talking about the points that are important, but in general you'll want to make sure you talk less and let them discover more.

Performance Games

Games like **Three-Headed Expert, Helping Hands, Foreign Film, Alphabet, New Choice,** and **Word Restriction** are the ones you might play in a typical short-form show. They usually have a teaching element to them. The kids adore these games and will ask to play them over and over again. What they like is the ability to show off their skills in front of their peers, and they like the magic of letting go and seeing the fun, and the creativity, that comes forth. They will repeat a clever line over and over for the rest of the class because they're just so delighted with themselves for being able to come up with it!

They will have a lot of success in these games if you set them up with exercises beforehand that help them learn the key components of the game they're playing. For example, **Three-Headed Expert** goes really well after you've had them tell a story one word at a time. Make sure you teach the components of the game in a safe and low risk way, so that they have experience with the concept before they reach the riskier space of performance. Be careful about piling on too many instructions at once—your kids may start to get overwhelmed and they won't be able to learn what you're teaching. This bears repeating—it's better to focus on one aspect of what they need to learn at a time. Gently bring in other challenges once they've got the basic concept. This way they will continue to be delighted with themselves and get excited about how much they have accomplished rather than overwhelmed by how much there is to learn.

During performance games it's also a great time to work on stage craft such as cheating out and speaking loudly enough to be heard. It's also a time to start talking to them about doing improv in front of an audience, to prepare them for what an audience might want to see and how to make them happy.

Example — Building a Yes, and Class

Now let's put together everything we've learned in this chapter. Here is how I built my class that focuses on "yes, and." "Yes, and" is one of improv's greatest concepts, but it's often misunderstood by kids and adults alike. For purposes of teaching and really understanding the concept, I find it easier to think of this as **acceptance and addition.** You'll see below that each element of the class is intended to set the kiddos up to discover this basic concept. Notice I said for them to discover. It's much easier to just talk to kids and tell them what is going on, but ultimately it doesn't work nearly as well. Set up a series of games and exercises through which they can discover what "yes, and" is and why it's important, and you will lead them to a fuller understanding of the concept.

1. **Bonding Games** — Get them ready to work together first. I like the **Sheet Game** for this because they acknowledge and identify each other in a fun and playful way. It leads to lots of giggling and the penalty for getting it "wrong" is super low.

2. **Warm-Up** — After that I want a good brain warm-up that gets them ready to accept each other. We do **Sound Ball,** which at some point may morph into saying words at the same time, or we let the kids mutate the game in any way that feels fun and full of acceptance. Often some of the kids will have a hard time with repeating the sound thrown to them. They just get so excited about the awesome noise they have pre-planned and they want to share it before they forget it. So you'll need to remind them to repeat first and after a few rounds they'll usually get it.

   Then we want to bring in the addition part of this lesson so we'll do **I Am a Tree**—acceptance is built into the game. They have to agree before they go out, and this game shows them how scenes are built by accepting and adding on to what is already happening. Also, I have never met a kid who didn't love **I Am a Tree**—they just eat it up and ask to play it over and over. You will need to keep reminding them to react to what's actually out there now, rather than pre-loading an idea and shoving that in no matter what else has been played.

"I am a tree"

"I'm a sailboat!"

When this happens, I'll ask them, "How does a sailboat fit with a tree?" Hearing their contorted justifications is absolutely hilarious! Eventually, they will calm down and do more reacting than pre-planning. But don't worry if this takes a while—it's just not easy for kids to contain their enthusiasm when they think of something that they love.

3. **Exercises —** I start with doing **No, But Parties**, where we discuss how nothing happens. Then we do **Yes, But Parties**, where a little more happens, and then **Yes, And Parties**, where fun and hilarity happen. I love hearing all the outrageous things they come up with. I like to challenge them—"This is improv . . . ANYTHING can happen!" I have seen kids develop parties with aliens, and waterslides from the moon, and famous pop-stars performing just for them. Then you'll have the child who just says "Everyone gets ice cream." I always think this one is going to be amazing at grounded improv someday.

   You do have to watch out for the kids who want to undermine what someone else has done. Like if someone says that Justin Bieber will play for them, and then another kid makes a face and says, "Yes, and Justin Bieber WON'T play." At that point you have to remind them that they have to accept what is happening—but they get to add anything they want to the party. This not only helps with improv, but also life. Being able to accept what is and then figure out how to creatively add to that and find your own joy is a pretty awesome skill to develop.

   These exercises are a lot of talk and brain work so keep it short or the kids will really start losing energy. We'll bring the energy level back up with **Where Have My Fingers Been?** This game forces them to accept the location and is also super high energy and silly. They really like repeating the chant, and moving their fingers around.

   Then we follow that with "yes, and" lines. In this one some kiddos will be excited to set up "funny" or "clever" offers. That's great. For this exercise, it's perfect to have a little show-off time—since fundamentally they'll need to accept what their partner says in order to complete the exercise, being clever won't ruin anything.

Other kids will blank out, and you'll need to let them take their time to find something. This can be hard—you watch their little faces contort as they search for anything they can say. It's important to give them a little time to find that answer themselves, but you don't want to let them hang so long that they start breaking down. If you think they need some help, you can give them a category to make it easier, like "Say something about the space you're in," or "What do you notice about that other character?" Or, "What does your character want?" This will give them a little structure to hang their offers on.

Often the kids will also get into a run of very similar offers. Most of the time it's "Look at _____." Or "Let's go ________." Once they discover these easy sentences, they don't want to try anything new. You can let this go for a little bit—remember we want them to feel successful. Then, when a child who is not super shy comes up, challenge them to change it up a bit. You can do this by asking them to start with a different word, or with something that's happening rather than something they see, or with something they notice about their partner.

4. **Performance Games** — In the last third of the class, open it up to teach performance games that use these concepts. That way the kids learn the skill and can immediately apply it in a game that shows how important that skill is.

   Alien Translation is a perennial favorite for pretty much all ages. In this one—you'll coach the "translator" to take the non-verbal offers of the alien to make them match up a bit. Often the "Alien," especially if you put a slightly controlling child in this role, will get upset at the "translator" for getting their words "wrong."

   "That's not what I was saying!"

   This is one of those teaching moments we're looking for, providing the opportunity to talk about accepting offers and working together. It will take a while but try to cycle everyone through all of the roles in this game so that they have a chance to play with these concepts.

Taxi works both acceptance skills and character skills and is great for the 9-and-up crew. Kids will often just repeat what the original character said, so coach them to stick to their character's concerns while also taking on the new character. This is super difficult for kids and is a great way to stretch and challenge them. I love this game because the kids will frequently play stock characters and it's delightful to see their interpretations of ones like the valley girl and the old man!

Creating Machines is delightful for the younger kids. It is very physical and lets them get the concept in their body, which is often a great way to short-circuit the brain. I like to make this super silly by waiting until all the kids are in the machine, then slowing it down or speeding it up, turning it sideways, or otherwise messing with them. If you end with it going so fast that it breaks down, watch out for kids collapsing in a pile of giggles!

Hesitation Debate and **Blind Line** will be challenging but exciting for the middle school and teens. They will have an easier time with acceptance, but need to be coached to add their own ideas as well. For this age group as well, you can use these games to introduce the concept of starting out slowly and then speeding up as you get later in the game.

Ultimately this "yes, and" class will let the kids feel the power of accepting and adding first. Then they get to play with the ideas directly and really sink into them and challenge them. And finally, they're rewarded for their hard work and effort by playing the performance games which have built-in rewards for meeting the addition and acceptance goals. This class will keep the kids learning, engaged, and encouraged.

Once you get the fundamental objective down, and a standard set of exercises, then you'll be able to easily adapt this to other types of classes—summer camps, workshops, etc. Creating these plans for your program, at least in the beginning, will be time-consuming and challenging, but it's a necessary component of a successful improv lesson. Also, it will keep you from having to play **Alien Translator** until your brain turns to mush!

CHAPTER THREE

GO! SETTING UP THE CLASSROOM

Picture this—the kids trickle into your classroom while you're still trying to figure out your plan for the day. They mess with the props you need and get into the paint that someone left out. As class starts, the same kids as usual are peeling the spike tape off the stage and one of the kids notices that there is a bird outside the window. This is not the way you want to start the day. You'll find yourself already frustrated and having to correct the kids a billion times before class even starts. How can you start a supportive, trusting class after that?

The environment of your classroom will make a huge difference in how you teach and how the students respond to your teaching. You'll want a space that supports the students in their exuberant, creative expression, but that's also safe and contained. You'll want the students to get context clues about what behavior is appropriate. Then they will naturally respond without you having to correct or direct them. They will feel safer knowing what they should be doing and where they should be. Children are often unsure about what they're allowed to do or what they're supposed to do, and the more you can guide them with a structured environment, the easier the class will be for them—and for you as a teacher.

No matter what kind of space you start out with or are given, there are many ways to create an environment that will support the students.

On the Way In

This is pretty obvious, but the first thing your kids will do is enter the room. If your teaching space is in a theater, then your job is pretty easy. Theaters are different from most of the spaces children inhabit, and they have a different feel from the outside or more familiar world. On the first day you'll need to give the kids some time to explore the space and ask questions. After that they will respond to the feel of the room and will come to order pretty quickly.

However, if you're in a classroom or gym, you'll need to do a little work to make it feel different. What you're aiming for is maximum difference between the space they've just left and the improv classroom space they've just entered. Can the lights inside be brighter? Can they be going from the outside to the inside, crossing a threshold of sorts? Is there a way that the transition can signal to the kids that they're now in a new space with new expectations?

"Time for Class!"

As you bring the students into the teaching space, you'll want to enforce the idea that they're entering a different world, not quite the same as the regular world they just left. One easy way to do this is have the kids gather outside the space and hold them there until the actual time of the class, then bring them in all together. This will create momentum and energy from the beginning. This also creates a subtle enforcement that the kids are a collective class, rather than a group of individual students.

The Hideout students usually gather in the cafe downstairs and say hello to each other. Then as it gets closer to class time they will crowd around the door to the upstairs, reinforcing and building on each other's excitement for class to begin. When we let them in, they will stampede up the stairs like a herd of tiny elephants.

Having them gather outside also makes it easier for the teachers to check in with the TA or other co-facilitators, to look over the curriculum, to make sure the room is ready, and to gather any supplies they may need for the class. This can be a very valuable moment, as it'll help the teachers get into the right headspace for the day. It also gives them time to prepare the space for the class without kids pulling on their attention. At the Hideout we frequently have to collect anything that might have been left by the adult classes the night before, like beer bottles or food wrappers. The kids love finding these, but I hate answering their questions about why people drink beer, etc.

If the children's parents have a place to gather outside as well, you have the added advantage of them starting to talk to each other. This will pave the way for playdates and other types of engagement outside of class. It's wonderful if the kids can form friendships outside of class—obviously friendship is a great thing in itself, but it's also perfect for creating troupes as they get to know each other better.

Unfortunately, there will always be stragglers. It is a sad yet inevitable part of childhood that kids don't have much control over things like being on time. That's up to the parents or caregivers, and they won't be coming in the room, so you want to be gentle with latecomers and understand that they're not being rude—in fact, it's more likely that they'll be really disappointed that they're late. That being said, you'll want to find ways to encourage being on time.

Often when a late kid comes in, the other kiddos in the room will often cheer for them, which can actually act as a subtle reinforcement for being late. If you can, discourage this without squashing the students' enthusiasm. If you're already discussing a game, don't stop to re-start the explanation. This makes it very boring for the kids who are already there and you'll lose a lot of the enthusiasm already in the room. Instead, just continue—often another kid will explain what the latecomer has missed. This sets up a sweet dynamic of the kids taking care of each other. If this doesn't happen, once the game begins, pull the latecomer aside and explain the game to them separately. Do this neutrally with no recriminations about being late. After all, they might have been struggling valiantly to get there on time and just missed, which happens to all of us. Missing out on the beginning of the game is enough of a repercussion for being late—you don't have to reinforce that with words.

If it does become a problem, it's okay to send the parent a note—although to be honest, I've rarely found this to be helpful. Mostly the parents will explain that parking is hard, or traffic was jammed, with no apparent understanding that if parking is always hard or traffic is always jammed, you could probably just leave a few minutes earlier. However, every once in a while, you'll hear a problem for which you can offer a solution, and then it's nice to make your parents' lives easier.

The Containment Room (Classroom)

The physical structure of your room will be the difference between kids who focus on you and what you're saying, and kids who can't stop themselves from playing with the stuff in the room.

You'll want a room that's large enough to play in and have fun, but with enough boundaries to keep all that energy contained. You'll want it to be interesting and a place that will support creativity, but if it's too interesting then the kids will be distracted and want to look at or play with things all the time. In the Hideout's space, we have curtains on the side of the stage. In every class of kids there will always be a few who want to wrap themselves up in the curtains and hide in them. Which I understand—it's really fun! However, it's also distracting and pulls the curtains down. So part of my prep for the space if I'm teaching kids younger than 10 is to tie the curtains into a knot so that they're higher and it's impossible for a young body to wrap themselves up in them.

If you have stuff in the space that's out of your control, then it's a good idea to set up a physical boundary. A row of chairs in front of something fascinating can be helpful. Or if you can find a way to cover interesting things, that's even better—maybe bring some old sheets! The term "out of sight, out of mind" was, I'm positive, developed for kids under 10 years old.

When you're able to anticipate and take care of these distractions ahead of time, your teaching becomes much, much easier and the students end up having a better time because they spend more time playing and less time being corrected.

In any improv classroom, you will need to have a large open area for play and gross motor movement. This often means moving chairs and tables—when you do that, you can use the chairs to form an audience and the tables to set up physical boundaries. This can make your classroom seem different from normal spaces and more like a stage.

Chairs make beautiful boundaries—one chair/one child is pretty much understood by anyone over the age of 6. Mats, squares, or circles on the floor are also generally understood to be one per child as well. This helps keep your audience neater and less likely to devolve into a massive pile of children on the floor. You will notice that I said "less likely." Many children are very touch-oriented and have a hard time keeping their hands to themselves. The younger they are, the more likely it is that they will roll on top of each other like a litter of puppies. The structure will help, but in some cases, you may just have to keep certain children separate from each other and accept that there will be some rolling and flopping.

You should also have a spot where you keep any props, supplies, pens, etc. If you always keep it in the same place, then the children will understand that these are yours. Younger children will be very excited by these things and want to see what you have today. They will likely have to touch them. You just have to accept that if you have something interesting lying around, the first few minutes of your class will be devoted to touching those objects and asking questions. If you don't want to spend time doing this or correcting this behavior, then your supplies will need to be out of sight, like in a box or bag, to be revealed at the appropriate moment later in class. Plus, the wide-eyed look when you bring out something like face paints, or masks, is totally worth it! It sounds like a small thing, but in a younger class this can make the difference between a really fun class with a special element, and a huge pain for you and lots of correction for them.

You'll want your kids to feel totally comfortable on stage—the best way to do this is to normalize the space. You do this by playing games, talking, and generally hanging out on and around the stage. Make it familiar and normal instead of foreign and scary. Then when it's showcase time they will already feel at home on the stage and can focus on their performance instead.

When?

You'll want to pay attention to the dates and times of your classes. They should be times that support the kids to be super successful and help make the parents' lives easier. Be aware that improv classes are considered an "extra" and parents are going out of their way to make sure their children can do this awesome activity. The more you can accommodate them, the more kids you'll have in your program.

Typically, kids follow a semester schedule—even homeschooled students are pulled into the semester structure by the culture around them. You can find the dates of the local school district online. Use these to determine your class dates.

The first week back to school is a mess, with parents figuring out their schedules and kids dealing with transitions. It's best to start your classes a week or two after they go back to school. That way they have a little time to figure out their lives before adding in improv. Be aware that the spring semester is often about a month longer than the fall semester, given the way breaks fall. If you make the class longer, it's good to explain to the parents that it's more expensive because of the extra classes.

Make sure to schedule time off around major holidays and school breaks. This will make it easier for parents to plan vacations and family trips. I remember the first year when I had a class over one of the Saturdays of spring break. I think only two kids showed up. That was not a fun class for any of us.

Classes should be weekly or, if you're doing a camp, daily. If you have classes less frequently than once a week, the children will forget too much in between—not just the improv you're teaching them, but also the rules of the class and maybe even their classmates. A weekly class seems like just about the perfect consistency to keep them going. It also fits very easily into most family schedules.

The length of class time depends largely on the age of the students. If the class is too short it will feel unsatisfying, but if it's too long you'll lose their time and attention.

The following is a good range of times based on the ages of the students.

<Age 8	45 minutes - 1 hour
8-13	1 - 2 hours
Teens	1.5 - 3 hours with breaks

In addition to the amount of time each day, you'll also want to look at when in the day the classes are held. Again, it's best to consider the rhythms of the kids and the needs of the parents. Your staff is also an important consideration. I've never had luck getting improvisors up to teach a 9 am class, ever.

For the 5-10-year-olds, catching them early means they're fresh and ready to go. So, look at the 10 am-noon time period if possible.

In the early afternoon most people experience a lull. This is more pronounced in younger children. If you do a class for younger children in the early afternoon, be aware that they'll probably need a few high energy warm-ups to get ready and shake off the afternoon doldrums.

For kids older than 10, an afternoon class is usually fine. Maybe add in some energetic warm-ups, especially if the class is right after lunch.

Teens have a hard time getting up early and will actually do better with a class in the afternoon or evening.

No matter what age your kids are, if you're teaching an after-school class, be aware that the kids have been focusing and concentrating all day. Starting with some big gross motor games will help them get the wiggles out before you start. Games with fewer rules and more running will be your friend here.

You will know that they need a break when they start getting super active in a way that looks uncoordinated and uncontrolled. At that point, sit them down for a snack if at all possible. Or find another way for them to rest and recharge such as drawing or listening to music.

Summer Camps

Summer camps, of course, will have a very different flow to them. Generally summer camps are at least a week long and cover most of the work day, making it easier for the parents to drop their kids off and pick them up around work schedules. Our camps are from 9-5, or if they're shorter they have "extended" times for people to keep their children there until 5. Occasionally someone will ask to extend times. I always ask one of my staff if they want to make some extra money for babysitting the kid until the parents pick them up. This is an easy gig, so finding staff isn't difficult. But I do make it clear that this is outside of the regular camp. They're contracting directly with the staff, so that I don't have to worry about normal liability concerns.

Because you'll have the campers for the full day, you have to pay close attention to the shape of the day. Improv is actually very exhausting and doing too much of it at one time will wear out your campers and their teachers. It's much better to keep the classes short and add in other non-improv elements.

Here are suggested class times for summer camp by ages.

< Age 8	45 minutes max
8-13	1 hour
Teens	1.5 – 2 hours

A good schedule for kids 8-13 looks like this:

9:00—9:15	Social time and gathering
9:15—9:30	Warm-ups
9:30—10:30	Class
10:30—11:00	Break for snack and social time
11:00—12:00	Class
12:00—1:00	Lunch and social time
1:00—2:00	Class
2:00—2:45	Movies/Rest time

2:45—3:00	Snack
3:00—4:00	Class
4:00—4:30	All classes meet to show some of the games they've learned
4:30—5:00	Just fun games, usually non-improv
5:00	Time to go home!

For the younger kids we keep the classes shorter and add in story times, craft times, and going for a walk.

The times for teens can be a little more flexible. I have found that teens don't want to get up early in the summer. Our Teen Intensives are only in the afternoon. Some parents have difficulty getting the kids there, but by the time someone is 14 or 15, they can usually figure out public transportation and, of course, the older teens can drive.

In summer camps it's pretty important to give the kids some unstructured time. That's why we have so many breaks. They need this time and space to allow for their own personal social styles. For instance, in this time period, some kids will just want to read or draw on their own. Other kids will want time to talk to friends and interact. Some will want to check in with grownups and get some attention from authority figures. All of this is good—the kids are figuring out how to meet their own needs. Downtime will also make your improv classes run much more smoothly. The kids who really want to talk will have had their socializing time and will be more able to focus on you and the class.

Because it's a very full and engaging day, the kids will need a resting break in the afternoon. We started showing a movie at 2:00 and suddenly we had fewer meltdowns and better focus for the last part of the day. We also got fewer complaints from parents about tired kids. Now the parents see that they're worn out at the end of the day, but they're not exhausted and unable to cope. It's much healthier for everyone involved.

If you see that many of your kids are crying easily, getting into fights, and just unable to focus, that's an indication the kids are overtired. In that case, maybe it's time for a calm sitting-down break, a discussion on some element of improv, a story, watching the teachers perform, or even just another break. Everyone will be much happier if you keep an eye on how much energy the kids have.

Overall, paying attention to the space and time of your classes will set you up for success before you even open the door. Once that's all done, then you can get to the fun stuff!

CHAPTER FOUR

THEY'RE HERE! NOW WHAT?

Teaching through games is a beautiful and useful way of getting kids to learn and retain information. It will make practicing key principles fun and exciting—the kids will beg to play certain games over and over again. This means they're getting something out of the game and it's engaging them. When games make the kids laugh and breathe and have a good time, these are perfect conditions for learning and retaining information. Different games will teach different skills or make the kids ready for different types of learning, so you'll want to pay attention to the sequencing of the classes as you develop your curriculum.

At the start of class resist the temptation to do a whole lot of talking. Kids really don't retain much from straight lecture or discussion. It's most fun and helpful to just jump in and play first and then explain either after they've been successful at the first couple of games, or sprinkle information throughout the play time. I mean, they probably won't need to know where the bathrooms are right at the start, so learning that information 10 minutes into class is really no big deal. Also, wait until you bump up against problems before you address them—this gives you a chance to show that mistakes happen often and are not a big deal. So if someone yells out that another child did something wrong, I like to say "Oh, I'm so glad you did that, now I have a chance to explain that we don't correct our classmates. Only the director can tell someone they did something wrong, and now we know that. Thanks for helping me point that out!" This way they're given the experience of doing something "wrong" and you're role modeling how you assess that, learn from it, and keep going.

The Shape of Each Class

You'll want to pay attention to how you set up the syllabus of your class. Each day should have a fair amount of variety—that's focus games, high energy games, challenging games, easy games, bonding games, and reflection time. Kids can have short attention spans, so switching it up frequently will allow them to follow their own natural structure. However, there are times when they will really dig deeply into something and the entire class will be captivated by a challenge or game. In that case it's fine to follow the natural flow of the individual class. Just know that when it's over, they will probably need something different. It's kind of like stretching after sitting for a long while—you just need to do the opposite for a bit to have a nice rest.

Don't Listen!

It is also good to let them play some with minimal supervision. I don't leave the room because children need to be supervised, but I'll go out of my way to make sure they know I'm not watching. This is especially easy in partner and solo games. I will look at my notes, examine something in the room, look anywhere but at them. You want them to have some time to figure this stuff out on their own. That way they have the room to make mistakes or play with the exercise without the pressure of getting it right or impressing you. It also gives them the chance to explore kid-level silliness without you correcting them or feeling foolish in front of you. Believe me, some kids really like talking about poop! Having a little time to do that when you don't appear to be listening is fun for them and helps them figure out how to be appropriate in different contexts.

Establish Questionable Authority

One of the dichotomies of teaching to kids is that you must be in control of the class and aware of safety—emotional as well as physical—at all times. However, to really let the kids discover in a meaningful way, you must also have a questionable authority that allows the kids to disregard you so that they can make their own decisions and discoveries. They need to learn to rely on themselves. And, if the kids feel empowered to take charge of their own improv, they will learn to rely on their own intuition instead of always looking to you to see if they're doing it "right."

Establishing authority is actually pretty easy and we'll go in depth with some of these concepts in Chapter 6, but here are some quick ways to get started:

- Calling them into a circle, and if they don't go quickly enough or make a good enough circle, making them go away and then try again until they perfect it.
- Don't explain all the rules of the class right up top, but instead, start with games first so they're a little off-balance and they have to look to you for the order of the class.
- Be decisive and concise when calling people to order.
- Make eye contact and call kids by name.
- Having them follow your directions that you give in a clear and simple manner will get them in the behavioral habit of following your lead.

However, in the realms of improv you want them to question you. They need to find their own voice and you want them to give you push-back on the concepts you're giving them so that they really understand them. Here are some ways to make the kids question you:

- When someone asks a question about which way to do a game, go ahead and try it both ways and ask the kids which one they like better. This might become your new version of the game.
- When kids push a game and do aspects that are wrong, but in the spirit of improv, go ahead and follow their lead and see what happens.
- When they ask "why" about something you're telling them, let them know you might be wrong, suggest they be willing to try it out, and ask them what seems better.
- When teaching new concepts, set up a scenario where they're going to discover it themselves and then let them tell you what they found. Write down their words from time to time. For example: when teaching "yes, and"—do the **No Party**, the **Yes, But Party**, and the **Yes, And Party**. Ask them what they got out of each one and when they might use these tools. List these tools on the board or on a big sheet of paper.

- Challenge them on a regular basis. This sets up the idea that you trust them and think they're capable. Even if it's a tiny challenge, label it as a challenge and get excited when they master it.
- Use the phrase "You're too good at this!"
- Challenge them to "break improv" whenever they're playing a new game.
- When mistakes happen, try seeing if that would be a good new variation. Ask the kids if they like it.

These are simply examples of ways to establish questionable authority without undermining your need to be the adult and to make sure the class runs smoothly. You can certainly continue to come up with other strategies—just remember that the kids still need to know that you've got them covered and they're emotionally and physically safe in the class.

Class Bond

It's important for the class to have cohesion. You'll want them to get along well and be able to work together to make the class run more smoothly. This is also important because improv classes are an important social time for many of the kids. They will often make good friends through these classes and this can become a very important and memorable part of their childhoods.

The goal is to turn them from a class of unrelated people into a class of friends. If you play bonding games at the start, it will begin the process of developing friendships. The very first aspect of creating unity is that you need to treat everyone as if they're a needed and valuable member of the class. This is paramount. You'll quickly see who's remarkably talented, intelligent, or charming. This is great and these kids are awesome, but the slower, more awkward, less capable kids have just as much to offer, and you'll want to go out of your way to treat them all as unique and important class members. The kids will look to you for how to treat other kids. You'll want to emphasize that everyone has strengths and weaknesses and all of their ideas are valuable.

Another way to make bonding happen is to show them they're all in this together. For example, when they get into the circle together and they have a hard time or take too long, go ahead and point out the people who got there quickly and correctly, but when you tell them to start again, they all need to work together. If they have trouble with this, point out the kids that are having a rough time and ask the others to support them in getting into the circle. It's amazing how well this works. Suddenly the slightly self-righteous kiddos will be helping the others, encouraging them and doing what they can to get everyone in place. You'll want to make sure there is no shame in your voice—this needs to just be a problem they're all solving together—let them figure out how to help each other. Sometimes a child will begin to chastise another child and that's the time to step in and remind them that they're there to support, not to criticize.

Another component of group bonding is to let them rely on each other. So, run a couple of kids through an exercise and then ask the other kids what they thought. You'll need to keep a careful reign on this—kids love to criticize—but if they start looking to each other to see how they're doing, then they will learn the components of working in a troupe. With the older kids give them "directing" practice, this helps them to start looking at ways to help others find their feet in a scene. It also gives them a chance to be involved and see a scene from the outside. In the long run it gives them insight into their own scenes.

You'll want to teach the kiddos to be supportive of each other—it seems like this should come naturally, but it really doesn't. So, if a child is struggling, go ahead and turn to the other kids and say "We all think you're awesome, even though you're having a hard time, right?" Phrased this way, the other kids will often start telling the child things they like about them and anyone who disagrees will likely keep quiet because of the peer pressure. Make a habit of applauding after scenes or games—and encourage all the kids to applaud—this will keep them focused on being helpful and supportive. In fact, even telling them to turn to their neighbor and give them a high five will make everyone feel good and get in the habit of supporting each other.

Showcases

Showcases are exciting and exhilarating! The kids have so much fun and it's delightful to see the parents be so impressed by their progeny.

With all the excitement, it can be easy to lose track of the fact that while this is a final project, it's not the focus of the class. It teaches important lessons and gives the parents an opportunity to see what their kids have accomplished. But don't put too much pressure on yourself or on the kids and focus on having a good time rather than making a perfect show.

Make It Special — Having a few extra special touches will make the whole thing much more fun for both the parents AND the kids. If you have a working theater, have them on the stage with the working lights and sound. Having house music going and the improvisors hidden as the audience filters in will give it a sheen of professionality. Include a little hosting and an actual light or sound tech and suddenly it feels like a real event!

If you don't have this setup, do what you can to still make it feel as legitimate as possible. Set up chairs in an audience, tape off the stage, have the improvisors off in a corner, have someone turning the lights off and on. All of these will mark this as a special occasion.

Before the Showcase — Take either two class days or two to three hours to really get ready for the showcase. You'll want to make sure the kids know and understand all the games and/or scene formats you'll play in the showcase. As you practice the games or format, keep track of who does well in which position so that when you make your set list, you'll know the best place for each kid. Don't share these with the kids unless they're super anxious about what they're doing—otherwise they'll spend two weeks planning this game and their performance will never live up to the expectations they develop in their heads. Also, make sure they know that they should be quiet on the sidelines and watch their classmates instead of getting distracted by conversation or fidgeting with things.

Transitions — Rehearsing the transitions is as important as rehearsing the games. You'll want to go through the hosting, how the kids come in, how they introduce themselves, where they sit, how they get on and off stage, what happens between games or scenes, how to handle chairs or any props and costumes, how the ending will happen, when they bow, and how they'll get back to their parents at the end.

If you'll be having lights and music, it's important to let the kids hear the music and see the lights first to get used to them and know what they'll feel like. After that, do all the transitions with lights and sound so they'll know how it will work in the show. The more the kids know and are secure before the show, the more they can concentrate on just doing the improv.

It's a Real Show — Treat the showcase like a real show and you'll end up with several advantages.

- The kids will feel really special and it will increase their self-esteem to see that their show is as important as a regular paying audience show.
- The kids will take the show more seriously and will be less likely to act too silly or mess up on purpose.
- The parents will enjoy it more and be impressed with what you're doing. They're more likely to sign the kids up again and recommend the course to other parents if they're impressed with what you're doing.
- AND it's really fun!

Hosting — Go ahead and offer a pre-show speech. There will be people in the audience who don't know what improv is, and it's great to let them know the kids are making this all up on the spot. Also, let them know to turn off cell phones—for some reason people often think that it's okay to keep their phones on because it's just a kids' show.

Let them know your policy on taking pictures or recording, but ask them to turn off the flash—first of all they don't need it and second, it's very distracting to the kiddos to have flashes going off. Let them know that clapping and whooping are appreciated and make the show better. Then, go ahead and introduce the troupe or troupes that will be playing. When they come on, have them say their names; this is the opportunity for them to have a credit for their work. And it starts the whole show off on a quick and positive vibe.

Outro — At the end of the show you'll want to make sure you cap it off. Introduce the teachers at the end and thank your tech people as well. The outro is also the perfect place to tell people about the next classes coming up and about any adult programs you might have as well.

What to Expect — There is this odd thing that happens—the kids will often forget much of what you have taught them. They will face the back of the stage, block each other, and speak softly. Just be aware that it's hard for them to maintain all the knowledge that they've learned while on the stage. It usually takes several performances for them to be confident enough to actually retain the lessons you've taught them. However, some kind of magic also takes over in these shows—suddenly with the lights and audience, whatever they say and do becomes much funnier and more interesting.

Heavily Direct the Show — You'll want to heavily direct the show. This way you'll keep the show on track and make sure that the kids have a fun time instead of dying on stage. So go ahead and tell them to face out, tell them to be louder, and even tell them what to do next in the scene. These little helps will make it a much more fun show for everyone, and to be honest, the audience will forget your remarks and just remember how brilliant their little darlings were.

Notes/Processing — During the show, make sure to keep notes about what's happening—what's working well and not so well.

After the Show — You'll only want to say positive things—the kids will be with their parents and will be anxious about how they did, so go ahead and tell them they did great as they leave, or say something specific about what you liked. If the parents say something negative, just point out the things you liked. Occasionally parents are embarrassed by their kids' behavior. Assure the parents that this is fine and normal and the kids are great. If there is a need for a heavier discussion, this is not the time for it.

During the Next Class — Go around and ask what their favorite things were about the show. Make sure to validate everything they share, and let them know that they did a good job. Then ask what were things that they wanted to change—just for themselves, or else you'll get a huge round of how other people messed up the show. Often when the kids reflect, they're very accurate in their assessments. You'll want to make sure you validate them as much as possible. They also are really hard on themselves, usually much harder than anyone else, so try to bring as much compassion to this class as possible.

Negative Feedback — The best way to deal with improv problems is to issue the kids challenges. It's not "You blocked your scene partners too much," but rather, it's "I'd like to see you be more open to your scene partner/s ideas. Your challenge is to really look at how much you can support other people's ideas." If you treat criticism this way, the child has something to work towards. Negative feedback can get into their heads and make it hard for them to be as light and easy as they need to be.

Overall the showcase can be delightful, exciting, and rewarding for the kids, parents, and teachers involved. Just keep the pressure low and the excitement high and it'll be a huge success!

CHAPTER FIVE

DIGGING IN: EXPLAINING GAMES AND EXERCISES

Learning how to explain, teach, and run games can be an artform in itself. Especially with kids whose grasp on language is a little tenuous. The advantage of teaching kiddos is that they're very receptive to learning new things and are usually willing to try things they don't totally understand. They also tend to be really excited about learning new things.

Physical

Look at the game first. Figure out if there is any physical component to the game. Kids are very physical and will feel more grounded and secure knowing how to move before they understand the concept of the game. So for **Woosh Bang Pow**, I show them the movements and have them copy them before I have them play with each gesture. This also makes it easy to direct any problems that come up immediately. For example, for the pow across the circle—at some point a child will turn that into a gun and shoot the person across the way. This is an excellent time to point out, in a playful way, that we don't shoot our friends in class. Or you can change the word "pow" to something that feels less gun-oriented like "Shazam!"

Most Basic Component First

Once you've figured out the physical component, then it's time to look at the most basic component of the game and teach that first. You need to break it down further than you would for adults. Kids really like mastery, and getting it right can be super important for them. But also, they seem to get confused more easily than adults and need to go a little more slowly and patiently.

For example, in **Woosh Bang Pow** I will have them send a woosh all the way around the circle first. Once they've all done that, I will introduce bang. I'll let them play with that until the woosh gets trapped between two kids who just want to bang it back and forth. Once that happens then I'll introduce the pow as a way to get out of the trap. Once we have pow, I'll often just have them send a pow around for a bit until it feels good to start up the game properly.

Once you've started this up, let it run and have fun with it, but also be willing to pull it back to its basic components again. One of the advantages of teaching in small, digestible bits is that, if the kids are having trouble with a portion of it, you can back up, play the easier component again until they really have it, and then try the new component again.

For example—in **Woosh Bang Pow** there are frequently kids who will only do bang, which is fine, but the poor child next to them basically never gets to play. So, it's great to take away the bang for a bit and then ask how it feels when it goes around with just whoosh and pow. That can also be a lot of fun. I'll also just take away bang from certain children, and only allow them to do woosh and pow, or even just woosh, so they get a better feeling of how to accept what's coming and be a part of the group.

Use the Fewest Possible Words

Most of this coaching should be done with as little explanation as possible. Unless there is a good reason for it, don't tell them why they're playing the game—let them discover it instead. When you're doing so much tweaking and breaking it into parts, it's really tempting to talk about each step, but don't do it! Just set it up and see how it all goes. If something needs to change—like a child will only do bang and so their neighbor doesn't get to play—just say, "Okay, you have a special challenge, you only get to play with woosh." Don't explain further, just watch them play with that and hopefully discover things as they go.

Kids really don't get as much information from speaking and when you start explaining things to them, they'll start fidgeting and lose concentration. However, when you just coach them into doing the thing that works best, then they will feel that in their body and will naturally gravitate to the thing that makes the game feel most fun for them.

Up the Level of Challenge

Once they've got the basics down, then it's fun to challenge them further. This can get incredibly fun as the kids love to be challenged and will delight at different renditions of the same game. With each game you play, you can find a way to deepen it or make it faster, or slow motion, or other things that just play with the fundamental concept. It's great to have the kids work with these different ideas because they will begin to see that nothing is set in stone. They will delight in playing these different aspects of the game and hopefully they will see that different improv tools bring different outcomes. The ultimate lesson from this is that in improv, nothing is wrong, it's just a different outcome and they have the freedom to explore these different outcomes and figure out what is fun for them in different contexts.

Hopefully at some point one of the kids will suggest an idea about how to mess with the game as well. This is a golden opportunity to let them take ownership of their improv! Even if you think it won't work, go ahead and try it and see what happens. It can be really fun for both you and the kids to see how it doesn't work and then figure out what to do to make it more fun. Or if it does work even better, then you can play that rendition as well. Make sure to credit the kid who came up with the idea to reinforce that they can make changes and propose ideas that will work.

Take the Blame

One situation that's pretty tough is when you have explained a game and they just don't seem to be getting it. Try to help them, but at some point, be willing to drop it if the trying is sucking energy out of the class. At that point you'll want to take the blame for the game not working. Kids are very attuned to failure and it can really freak them out unless it's handled gently. So just let the kids know that you're having a hard time explaining it well, or that it worked when you saw it someplace else, and you'll have to figure out what you're doing wrong so it's not working here. I usually give a huge failure bow at that point to reinforce the concept that failure is okay and everyone does it. Just as long as you let them know it's not their fault and they didn't do anything wrong. This also role models that it's totally okay to not be right or perfect all the time. Then, as quickly as possible, switch to a game that's very easy to master. This gives them a boost of positive energy.

If you do decide to come back to the same game, maybe on a different day, attack it with excitement, and let them know it should go easier this time! Feel free to laugh about how badly it went last time—again making it your own fault, and let them know that you've figured out how to change it to make it better. Assuming it does go better this time, then it can be really useful to ask the kids why it was better/easier this time. See if they can start using their critical thinking skills in this instance to see what and how games work.

Explain at the End

Wait until the game is done before you give an explanation of why you did the game. And this is really not a necessary step because they don't actually need to understand a game to get the benefit from it. In fact, you don't want to get the kids in their heads too much and focused too much on "rules." Kids are very rule-bound and erasing rules is a great way to give them freedom to play.

When you do explain games, make sure that you're using vocabulary they can understand. You'll need to adjust significantly for the littlest kids of course, but even the high school kids have a smaller vocabulary than your average adult. They often won't say anything if they don't know a word because it's very embarrassing to them not to know a word, and they usually try to pick things up from context.

Kids do well with metaphors, so try coming up with something that's familiar and work from there. One of my favorite examples: When I'm explaining why you need to accept and add to offers, I'll say, "It's like when you build with Legos or blocks. If you put down the first Lego, which is an offer, and then I come along and knock it off, which is blocking, then you have to start over. Can you do it? Yes. Is it fun? No. So let that first Lego—the offer—stand, and then add another brick. Then you can build and build and build—either you end up with a beautiful tower, which is like a scene. Or you can wait until it's really tall and THEN knock it over, denying the reality of the scene, and then it's super fun and funny." This is a much more visual way to explain the process of building a scene and will help kids see it in a familiar context.

Learning how to explain, teach, and run games can be an artform in itself. Especially with kids whose grasp on language is a little tenuous. The advantage of teaching kiddos is that they're very receptive to learning new things and are usually willing to try things they don't totally understand. They also tend to be really excited about learning new things.

CHAPTER SIX

RUNNING THE CLASS: HOW TO MANAGE THE KIDS

Once you've got your curriculum and you understand how to implement it, then it's time to meet the kids and see how it all works with them. No matter how much you prepare, you need to be flexible when you're in front of actual children. They will always surprise you. There are several strategies that will help you make the classroom run more smoothly and make sure everyone, including you, has fun.

Physical Environment

As discussed in Chapter 3, it's much easier to run a classroom that's set up correctly. The most important thing here is to make sure that you don't have anything unsafe in the environment and that as little as possible is off limits. This is obvious for the little ones, but honestly even the high school kids have a hard time avoiding interesting temptations. You'll be explaining the rules of the next game to them and then one of them will unconsciously reach out to play with the curtains that hang from the side of the stage—that you already asked them to stay away from. It's like they don't even realize they're doing it! It will distract you and the other kids and you'll have to make the decision to correct them and interrupt the flow of what you're doing, or let it go and make it more likely that the other kids will also start playing in the curtains. Make the environment safe and secure with minimal distractions and you won't have to correct the kids over and over. This will keep your classroom more positive overall.

In addition, try to make your learning space feel contained. Define a play space and a separate audience space. This creates comfortable boundaries and helps the kids adjust their behavior based on their physical location. Kids do well with physical, concrete boundaries, so having a cue for where they're up and moving, and where they're sitting quietly really helps them transition between loud and bouncy, to still and focused.

Establish Order Within Chaos

For the children to learn and grow, there has to be a fair measure of space and behavioral latitude. For the games to go well and your classroom to be a place where they can learn, there has to be a certain amount of control. Negotiating this dichotomy between chaos and order is part of your fundamental work as an improv teacher. You will get better at this the longer you teach. However, there are some good tricks for making order happen without dampening the curiosity of the students.

Make Good Circles — Since the standing circle is the beginning of so many improv games, go ahead and take time to make this a good platform to build on. The kids will often make strange ovals or weird blob-like creations as they come together—some of them clumped together, the shy kid hanging back so you can't really see them and the exuberant kids coming forward so that they can dominate the game as much as possible. When this happens, it's time for circle practice—let them mill about, pretending to talk to each other—then call out "circle up" and count to 5 and see if they can make a good circle by 5. It usually takes a few times before they can do it well. But the exercise in itself is pretty enjoyable, and the tension between ignoring what's coming and then racing to make it work is fun for kids. So, it's likely they will be pretty willing to work on this until they're happy with the results.

Managing circles does two things. First of all, a good circle will serve you well in making the game work. But also, it reinforces that you're in charge of the structure of the class. This helps psychologically because as the kids play with other boundaries, they will feel secure in the fact that you're able to keep them contained.

Keep Them Off Balance — This only works in the beginning. When kids don't know what is happening, they will naturally and automatically follow the structure of the adults. In the beginning, use this to your advantage. Don't tell them all the rules right away. Make them play games without explaining them and then explain the boundaries only as they come up. Again this does two things: 1) it makes the kids look to you to figure out what's going on, which establishes a habit of them looking to you for structure and 2) it gets them more comfortable with being unsure and not knowing what is going on, but in a safe and secure environment. This is a fundamental improv lesson.

Attention-Getters — Having a signal that means "it's time to be quiet and pay attention to me now" is very important. This way you'll spend much less time yelling over them, which is an unpleasant way to deal with people anyway.

You want to establish this in the first class, towards the beginning. The first time everyone starts talking, or you're in the middle of a game, and need to come back to order, bring up that you'll need a way to get their attention. It will feel less condescending to the kids if you bring up the subject this way, because it's more obvious why you need an attention-getter and they can help decide that this is an important thing to have in class.

It will work better, and be more fun, if your attention-getter is something that they help create, or at least agree with. Oftentimes, when you bring up that you need an attention-getter, the kids will excitedly tell you how they do it in other classrooms. As a class you can decide on one of these or make up one together.

Make sure that there is some component of them reacting, giving a response to your call. That is how you will know you have their attention. Also, if they have to make a noise, that will interrupt their current talking and help other kids come to attention.

Classic Attention-Getters

1. Clap the rhythm of "shave and a haircut," and have kids clap back the "two bits" part.
2. You clap a rhythm and the kids clap back the same rhythm. (This can get fun and silly as you go to more and more elaborate rhythms using different body parts.)
3. Sing the first part of the commercial jingle "We are Farmers" and the kids sing "Badedum dum dum dum dum."

4. Say "do what I'm doing" while making a movement—like patting on my head. The kids then mimic it. This is great when you want them to move to something quieter and works well with the 5-8-year-old crowd.
5. There is an attention-getter you'll hear about, but I don't recommend it: Hold up a certain number of fingers and wait quietly until the kids see you, hold up their fingers, and get quiet. I don't recommend this because there is usually a pocket of kids who are talking excitedly and then I either have to call them out, or they realize that they're the last quiet ones. Either way it seems pretty embarrassing, and even becomes a punishment for being enthusiastic about something. Enthusiasm is not something we want to punish.

Establish Yourself as the Fun Leader — Make sure that you're having fun. Whatever you do, be passionate and enthusiastic about it so that you can communicate that tone to the kids. Obviously, this works well with the little kids; their enthusiasm tends to overflow. But also make sure the older kids know that you're loving this. You're loving the games and improv and teaching, and by extension them. In this way, the kids realize that you hold the key to fun and excitement, and they'll be much more ready to follow you.

Control the Structure, Not the Content — When introducing a game, make sure you're rigorous in its structure. Coach the kids through each piece of it and make sure they fully understand it. But then let them go as much as possible. You don't want to let them get offensive or hurtful to each other, but other than that let them play and really discover their own sense of humor. I start **Sound Ball** with only noises, but then let it evolve into words. When it gets too cumbersome, I'll ask the kids why it's not working right now. They will usually say it's taking too long to think of things or too long to say things. Then we recommit to just letting sounds fall out of our mouths and not being clever. This gives them ownership of their own experience and is fundamental for their growth as improvisors.

Start Off Structured and Then Let It Go — Get the game, scene, format really established and then loosen up and allow them to play with it. Often the kids will come up with delightful changes to the basic structure. Sometimes this will even evolve into a new game.

Give Tiny Lectures — When it's necessary to have them sit down so you can explain something, realize that this is a very specific way of interacting that often will put them in "school mode." This is a very top-down way of giving out information and sets you in a very authoritarian space. Because of this I try hard to make sure that I undercut that authority. I make fun of the fact that I have to give a lecture and roll my eyes—"Ugh! Lecture time." I call them Teeny Tiny lectures. I set my timer for two minutes and try to get everything in under that time. The kids love this game, but more importantly they tend to listen when I make it obvious that the only way I can get the info across is in lecture format and that I will only impose this lecture on them for the shortest time possible.

A few years back I remember thinking to myself that kids in general were just getting better. I mean, they just seemed nicer and kinder and easier to deal with in classrooms and there were fewer of "those" kids who make teaching so difficult. It took me a bit of time to realize that actually, it was mostly that I was becoming much better manager of the classroom and that the kids were responding with cooperation and creativity. Actually, I also think this next generation of kids is going to be pretty awesome—but that's a different book!

Managing kids in the classroom is something that takes time and close attention to master. These strategies will help you on the road and give you tools to use when you encounter problems. But alas, nothing helps you out more than lots and lots of experience.

However, once you have a perfectly loose but appropriately firm structure established, the kids will really have both the freedom and security to play and discover and create. It becomes a super fun classroom that everyone is excited about joining each week, which makes your job easier and much more delightful!

CHAPTER SEVEN

ONE OF THESE THINGS IS NOT LIKE THE OTHER: TEACHING TO DIFFERENT AGE GROUPS

You'll find pretty quickly that kids are very different in their abilities according to age. Some of the fundamentals in improv are simply developmentally inappropriate at some ages, whereas you'll be surprised by how easy some things come to the kids at other ages.

What you'll want to strive for is hitting the things the kids are good at at their age—strengthening those skills so they don't fall off as much when the kids go through the crucible of adolescence.

You'll also want to introduce concepts that are age inappropriate, that really stretch the abilities of the age group of the children, and give them a little time playing with those concepts so they have a base of knowledge and vocabulary when they do reach a stage where they can incorporate that into their play. Just make sure to introduce these inappropriate skills in a way that doesn't feel stressful, and always strive to give the kids a positive experience so that they retain their joyful play and excitement for the work. Letting them know this concept is something they'll explore more as they become older will provide a challenge for them (because kids are always wanting to do what older kids do!) without making them feel like failures if they don't quite get it yet.

Ages 5-7

To understand this group, you'll have to realize that these kids are so wrapped up in their own development and their own world that reaching them with your communication and getting them to focus can be really difficult. In this group you'll spend a lot of time bringing them back to socially appropriate behavior. The kids rarely WANT to misbehave, it's just that their brains are too wired in the present moment to keep any instruction or direction in their heads for long. But it also means that working on being in the present moment will go really well. They don't even know how to plan ahead for the next move in the story, so exercise and praise their ability to go with the flow.

Strong Authority — Kids this age need a strong and compassionate authority figure to feel safe. They know that they're very vulnerable and in a world that they don't know how to navigate alone. They need the adults in their lives to be strong and capable so that they can feel comfortable playing and exploring.

The kids will believe, respect, and quickly love you with very little effort on your part. If you tell them to do something they will likely try to the best of their ability. If they don't follow directions it's probably because they can't, so it's time to look for the underlying cause of the behavior.

Emotions — The 5-7-year-old kids don't have a filter on their emotions. Everything they feel comes out immediately and intensely. If they're sad, they cry. If they're angry they will yell or hit. If they're happy they will giggle and jump up and down.

So, they're great at having strong reactions to things. These reactions are not super nuanced, but they're big! This is an important thing to work and praise, especially with girls, because as they get older, they will be told over and over to tone down and mitigate their emotions. If you've given all your kiddos a time and place where strong emotions are not only allowed, but valued, then they will retain some of their ability to call that up—even as they're being trained to be more socially appropriate "good girls and boys" outside of class.

Storytelling — The 5-7-year-olds are natural and proficient storytellers. They love reading stories, they love acting out stories, and they love telling stories. You can spend most of your time in class just on these three activities and the kids will be happy and be learning tons of improv skills.

They will often tend towards telling the same types of stories over and over again, so it's fun to stretch them. Read a story to them—a classic means that they will probably already know and love it—acting it out from the book at first. Once you've done that, start brainstorming different ways the story can go and then act that out. This uses the skill they already have and love—storytelling—to stretch their skills of being flexible, to allow new ideas to pop up and then go with the flow, which is not super natural to kids this age.

You telling stories and having them act them out will develop their skills for listening and following along—skills which are hard at this age. They will often want you to change the story to something they like better—but stick to your story! They need to practice the skill of following as well as leading.

Some of them, but usually not all, will love telling stories and having the other kids act them out. It's kind of magical to see a child spin a story and see his peers bring it to life. They will often have a very flat story arc, with maybe more adventures than conflict and resolution. But that's okay—the important thing is that they develop the confidence to tell their stories and see how they actually work when being acted out live and in the flesh.

Same Characters — Because of their need for repetition, you'll find that the kiddos will want to be the same character or types of characters over and over again. Let them be their stock character once or twice as they do love it and it makes them feel more comfortable, but then feel free to stretch them. For instance, if a child only wants to play puppies in every story, then she can be a puppy, but try a variation—maybe she's a puppy who sad because she doesn't have a person to love her. Or a puppy who is very selfish and doesn't want to share her toys. This way the child will end up exploring a fuller range of emotions, but within the comfort of her favorite character. Reading other stories will also help kids stretch—for example, if you have a book that doesn't have a puppy in it, this child will figure out which other character she wants to play. Sadly, just you making up stories that don't have a puppy in them doesn't work well, as a child like this will probably just demand to be a puppy or turn whatever you try to make her into the dog version of that!

Costumes, Dance, Art, Etc. — These kids don't have a real distinction between one kind of art and another. It can be great to bring in other disciplines to expand your lessons. Costumes help them flesh out their stories and they have a blast with them! If you buy pieces that are not very obviously one type of character, then the kids will use what they have and get creative about making them into what they need for the story. I love seeing how unselfconscious the kids are as they weave capes and scarves around their bodies to come up with their perfect outward representation of what they feel inside.

While the kids this age just can't get rhythm games yet, they do love dance and will enjoy games like **Dance Diamond** or **Freeze Dance.** These games will exercise skills around moving the body while also listening to instruction, so they're a great way to extend skills.

Similarly, there will be days when big, energetic games don't feel like a good idea. For these I like to bring out paper and markers. **Eyes on Paper** is great if the kids can get the idea that they have to take turns. You can get rolls of art paper at the craft stores—have the kids lay down while a friend traces them. Then they use their body outline to create a completely different character.

There are many other types of disciplines you can bring in—the important thing with this group is just that they enjoy their creativity.

Repetition — At this age they will need and love to play the same exercise and game over and over again. It is always shocking to me how long and often kids this age will beg to play the same game.

However, this is actually really good for them. If you remember that they're still wrapped in the cocoon of their own developing minds, then you realize that for any lesson to stick, they'll need to do it over and over again.

Fortunately, they tend towards the games that teach them or exercise skills that they need to work on for their own development. So feel free to play these games as often as you can stand it, knowing that they kids really are getting something out of the repetition.

The only problem comes in when one child loves a game but another is bored by it. This usually means that the first child is still working on this skill but the second child has mastered it and is ready to work on something else. So, this can be a great place to work on taking care of your partner—which is not a developmentally appropriate skill, but one that needs work anyway.

Rules are Hard — At this age, they're learning so many rules to so many things in their lives outside of improv that it seems they have no room left over for really getting the rules to games. Although they will try, they have a really hard time understanding and keeping up with new rules. Most of the improv games that you know will have to be stripped down to their most basic components to be taught successfully. So, play the games, but just remember to make them super easy and be ready to coach with positivity to keep them on track.

Distractions — Kids at this age are very easily distracted. It's the downside of being constantly in the present moment. If they see something shiny or think of something funny, they will focus on that totally until it loses their interest.

The best way to deal with this is just to handle distractions as quickly as possible. If kids are touching or looking at an interesting object in the room, remove it or hide it. If one of the kids has an unusual hat or outfit on, the kids will have to comment on it and explore it before they can focus on anything else. New people or things in the room need to be introduced and explained before you can go on with any lesson. As long as you deal with distractions instead of trying to ignore them, you'll be just fine.

Touching — These younger kids have a strong need for touch—some more than others of course. But some kids seem like they almost can't stop themselves from touching other kids and you. You'll need to decide what level of touch you're comfortable with for your class. For instance, some places won't let children sit in an adult's lap and discourage hugs.

No matter what you decide, these kids will need some kind of appropriate touch, so maybe hand-holding, or back-rubbing. There will be times when they're scared or anxious and will need to hold onto you—it's important to find a way they can do this appropriately so they don't feel rejected.

Also know that no matter how lax you are, the kids will still violate your boundaries at some point, just because they don't have a good understanding of appropriate physical boundaries. When that happens, just move their body to a more appropriate position, gently and with no remonstration. They will understand being moved better than being told anyway. Just make sure to do this without any shame as you want to make sure the kids don't develop an unhealthy perception about touch in general.

When dealing with them touching other kids, it's good to have a short and gentle phrase that you can use such as "Keep your bodies to yourselves." However, no matter how much you say this or how strongly you set the boundary in the first place, some kids will not be able to follow it consistently. Again, this is just their developmental stage, so remember that you're asking them to stop something that's totally necessary anyway in their development.

Ages 8-10

This group is wired for figuring out the world and their place in it. In their minds, everything has rules and some kind of order—they just have to figure it out and they'll be safe. They know that there are subtleties in the world of social interaction and don't yet know how to navigate them, but are trying to get it. They're super bound by rules, and at the same time they love breaking rules. It's like they're constantly challenging the boundaries of the world so they can understand how far they can go. Unfortunately, most of them can only figure that out when they go too far and are pulled back.

This age is the golden age for short-form games. They get the rules, and they love playing with when to break them and when to stick to them. If you keep the scenes short, the kids will really excel at this type of improv. Their natural energy and playfulness will bring out the fun of these games.

Ride the Chaos — For the 8-10-year-old kids, your job more than any other is to ride the chaos of the class. These kids have energy and enthusiasm! Although some of them have discovered the power in being negative and pouty—they will tell you they're tired, but often they just want attention. They don't understand most of the subtle social cues, with each other or with you, but it's a great age for exploring total silliness and just going to the extremes. This group will often end scenes by flailing their arms, running around in circles, falling down, or screaming. Let as much go as you possibly can. They're on the cusp of learning that they must be better behaved to fit into society and in the next several years their self-esteem will take a beating and many of them will start to figure out ways of dealing with that, ways healthy and unhealthy. So at this age, before they're under attack, spend as much time as you can delighting in their antics and letting them play hard and discover what's fun about themselves and their own brand of humor. When you do reel them back in—for example these kids love toilet humor and will always go too far with it—make this about what is appropriate in context, not that they've done something wrong or that they're bad somehow. I often say, "Okay, that's the type of joke you tell your friends, not something the grownups in the audience will like." This helps them figure out that context is part of being appropriate.

Yourself as a Fun Provider — This group is less concerned with safety—they now know they can get along in the world and they don't need their hands held as much. Your main job with them is to convince them that you can deliver the fun in class.

With these kiddos you can't start with the rules, because they will get bored and will settle themselves into class mode—which is not what you want. Instead, we always start in a standing circle and, always, even on the first day, start with a game that I know they can accomplish easily. Once we've got that down, then I can make announcements and tell rules and figure out names and anything else I need.

At this age, when you do your focus call and response and they keep talking, appeal to the fact that we're all wasting time that we could be spending on games. This actually works for a bit, but the kids will still want to talk. They can't stop the comments and bits—they tend to know that bits are funny and they want to have that attention, however, they have no idea when to stop! I will actually train them in this—one bit's funny, two bits starts to be irritating, three bits is disruptive and almost every teacher will stop you there. This helps them to start gauging when humor is helpful and when it will be unappreciated. (A lesson many adult improvisors could also use!)

Pull Them Up Short — Because these kids are so energetic and chaotic, they will often need some redirection. Start first with the standard ways of talking to kids: "It's time to be focused now, watch your body space, be careful with your friends." This works for about 2/3 of the kids. For the other 1/3, this will not work consistently. These less compliant kids often push on authority. If it feels like the kid is trying to follow directions, then stay easy and gentle with them. However, when you get the feeling that they're pushing on the authority boundary, and playing with how far to go, then it's time to reel them in, meaning you let them know they have gone too far, because this is often all they really need. Make sure the consequence is swift (and short), that there is no discussion, and you use as blank a face as possible. One of my favorites is "You need to sit down for one minute, you count it out, you can come back when you get to 60." Then look away from them and go back to whatever else it is that you were doing. This gives them something else to concentrate on for the one minute. It is a very short punishment, but it lets them know that what they're doing is going too far. Another way is to get lower so you're on their level, make strong eye contact, and with the same blank face say "I need you to stop that right now, do you understand?" This forces them to respond. Again, this is only for the kid who is testing boundaries because you want to let them know they've gone too far. The kid who just forgets or is too exuberant will not be able to stop himself and so just needs the constant gentle reminders.

Rules — These kids LOVE rules and are wired to do a great job with understanding what they're supposed to do, though not always why. This is why you end up with so many amazing chess champions who are so young—their brains are wired for understanding the rules of the game. However, kids also love breaking rules and seeing what the reactions are. This is fantastic for teaching short form games. The rules to things like **Alien Translator**, or **Good Bad Worst Advice** will give them a structure to play in and it will make them feel much safer, and consequently their improv will be much better. Any game with a fair amount of structure will be really fun for them. And they will almost always look for ways to break the game. Encourage this! This is a great way to find funny beats or to discover a new game. For example—in **Good Bad Worst Advice,** someone will discover that they can be a non-speaking character like a dog, and just bark their advice. This is fun for them, and they feel super clever having figured this out. We want to encourage them to push these boundaries and find alternate ways to see the scenes and the world.

Because the 8-10-year-olds are so rule bound, they will often find something funny and from then on, see it as a rule for how you get a laugh. They will then do that bit over and over again—the younger ones will repeat it right away, while the older ones will try to do that scene again week after week, just so they can insert that same funny joke. While this is fine for a while, and even understandable, you'll need to encourage them to find new ways to be funny. They can do it, it just takes exploration. Let them know this is a great tool to have in their funny tool box, but it can't be the only tool, and they can't use it for everything.

Simple Games — These kids will love to play games and really relish the fun of following and breaking rules, but for the most part they will have a hard time with the more scenic games. So, try for things that are heavily rule-based, but don't have too much unstructured space. For example,

Three-Headed Expert, Taxi, Slideshow, Alien Translator, and **Fortunately Unfortunately,** will all work well. As they get more and more able to handle time and space on stage you might try **Bus Stop, Elevator, Pan Left/Pan Right,** and **New Choice.** However, with these you'll still need to really stay on top of it as a director, coaching them as they go. Be willing to keep these games short. You'll find that the kids will have a natural range that they can do well in, usually about 2-4 lines, and then they'll get scared and start to either scream and flail their hands around or just shut down. At this age, part of your job is getting them to stretch that 2-4 lines as far as they can. Don't have super high expectations here—even just a few more lines will make them look and feel brilliant!

Touching — These kids will be varied in their need for touch. Some of them will want to wrestle and embrace one another frequently, and others will really want their space. This sets up a situation that can be difficult for everyone. The kids who want to touch are often the ones who are a little less mature and more high energy. You might describe this as "boy energy," but be aware that about 10% of girls have this same energy. These kiddos will hug and wrestle and fall on other kids all the time because they love and long for the sensation of touch with their friends. It's one of their communication avenues. So, you'll need to remind them frequently to keep good boundaries, and to respect their friends' needs for space.

However, this does set them up for being really good at games where they have to touch. These kids will do great at things like **Helping Hands, Moving Bodies,** and as they get older, even **Touch Talk.** You'll want to make sure they don't feel bad for this—it's part of their latent sexuality and you really don't want to shame them here.

Police — Kids this age also really really like to police each other. Because they're so rule-bound, when other kids break the rules, it bothers them extremely. It's not just because someone else is getting away with something, but because it's wrong and they can't handle the complexity of someone being wrong and letting it slide while they work on something else.

So, you have to do some reminding that you're the teacher and you'll handle the correction. I usually try to bring this out in **Category Die**. We'll be going along and one kid will get away with something that isn't really in the category and then someone else will call it out. I use this as a chance to explain that, first of all, you don't look good to your peers or the audience if you call out one of your friends on stage. You look like you care more about the rules than you do about your friends. (I mean, this is usually true, but part of being a social person is pretending that you're more mature than you really are.) But also, I explain, when a kid breaks a rule, it's like the kids against the director, and so if one of you gets away with something, it's like all of you win. The kids like this aspect of it, because they really like getting away with things. It also reaffirms that they need to be on the same side and working together and gives them this tiny skill for how to do that.

This dynamic is something you can use as well. The kids will really enjoy being the ones to run **Category Die** and call people out. In fact, pretty much any game that has someone who calls out anything will be fun for these kids. They really love being in charge and making other kids do what they say. Just remember to keep this in check by making sure they don't abuse their power, and teaching them how to be a good leader in these games.

Arguments — Probably because of their black and white view on the world, these kids end up getting into a lot of arguments. Most of the time these arguments don't really have any real basis in anything serious. They just both really want to be right. You have a few options here, which are all valid.

If you're in the middle of something else and don't have time to meditate, it's totally fine to just separate them and tell them they can't argue right now. They will probably glare at each other and harbor bad feelings for a while, but often will forget the argument in 5-10 minutes.

If you have time, or if the argument seems significant enough that you want to devote time to it, then you, or an assistant, can mediate it. The standard mediation technique is:

1. The first person names the problem and the emotions they're feeling, using "I" messages if possible. ("I don't like it when you always make me a dog in the scene.")
2. The second person listens and reflects back the statement. ("You don't want to be a dog anymore.")
3. The second person states what they feel the problem and emotions are, still using "I" messages. ("I really like dogs and I don't like it when you won't be a dog.")

4. The first person reflects back what they heard. ("You want me to be a dog in scenes.")
5. Then they brainstorm solutions and come to a resolution. ("One of us can be a dog and the other person can be the dog's owner.")
6. If they can't come up with something themselves, then the adult will help work this out.
7. If they still can't come up with a resolution, then they both sit out of the game until they can come up with something they agree upon.

Doing this will help a lot with settling arguments, but you have to have time and energy for this. Don't go into this if you're feeling resentful or angry yourself. If you are, you'll need to put this off until you've calmed down as well.

However, no matter how well you handle them, arguments and conflict will occur. Think of it this way—these kids only have a few years of figuring out interpersonal conflict without their parents, so of course many of them are not great at it yet. Even the really mature kids will occasionally have conflicts—that's just the nature of this age.

Girl/Boy Split — A notable characteristic of the 8-10-year-old crowd is that these kids, more than any other, will divide themselves along gender lines. Many of the kids will not be happy if there are mostly kids of the other gender. They will only partner and choose groups with people of their own gender. This always strikes me as weird because to be honest, this seems to be the most genderless age, besides toddlerhood. These kids tend to dress the same, they do the same activities, they're often similar in behavior, but still they feel this deep need to take a stand for their gender.

It's best to let them feel comfortable in these groups, but then to also make them choose other partners from time to time. When we divide up for games, I let them do whatever they want for the first one, and for the next, say they have to pick a different partner. If I continue asking them to pick different partners, eventually they'll be forced to have a partner of a different gender. When this happens, sometimes the girls, but almost never the boys, will make faces, and disgusted noises. Don't let this continue. Remind them they have to be respectful of everyone regardless of their gender.

Best Friends — Related to this topic, often you will have a set of best friends—two kids who only want to partner with each other. Oftentimes, even though they don't mean this, it can end up being hurtful to the other kids in the class, especially other kids of the same gender. They feel rejected and like they aren't good enough to be friends. Deal gently with all of this. Best friends are a beautiful thing to have, especially at this age, but encourage them to partner with others, and to be kind to others even as they express their love for each other. Encourage the kids who are left out to make friends in the rest of the class. Let them know that the two best friends are just really happy with each other right now and don't mean to be rude or exclusionary—it just comes off that way. This is usually a problem that settles with time.

Ages 11-13

Please be aware that these kids are going through some really rough times. Girls will typically go through puberty a year or two early, so in most of your classes you will have tall, adult-looking girls and shorter kid-looking boys, but they're still the same age. Puberty can be really difficult on just about everyone and you never really know what's going on with these kiddos outside of classes. Also, kids are at very different maturity levels as well—some will stay stuck in the 8-10-year-old mind frame until they're 13 or so, and some of them will instead shoot forward really quickly. Handling a class with these different levels takes some finesse!

This is where you'll start getting bizarre behaviors that seem malicious or cruel or unhealthy. This is the age group where people start creating their coping mechanisms to deal with the fact that their needs and what the world gives them doesn't always match up. Some kids develop healthy coping mechanisms; however, many of them do not. For the latter kids, they have to practice getting it wrong over and over again before they can possibly stumble upon getting it right, and finding a healthier way to cope. As difficult as it sounds, improv can be a saving grace for many of these kids, because of its attitude about failure. Continue pointing out that failure is natural and just a part of life, that what they have to share is important, and that you believe in them, and you will make such a big difference in the lives of your pre-teen kiddos.

They're also playing with identity factors now. Who they are now starts being defined in relation to their peers and the world around them. Pre-teens will dress one way for a while then may change radically to try a new style. Improv class is a fantastic place for them to start playing with this and to really dig into who they are and how they want to be seen.

At this age, kids are all about their peers. There are lots of status shifts and lots of changing friendship groups. This makes this a perfect age to work on all the social aspects of improv such as bonding, status, taking care of your partner, etc.

Work — Some kids this age are starting to really want to work on more in-depth improv. These are generally the more mature kids. They want to get to the harder parts of scene work, and play the games that have more scene work in them. Be aware though that their ability to pull off nuanced, grounded improv work is hampered by their current brain formation. They literally don't have the developed brain to work on some of the emotional aspects that they want to work on, so generally they play very two-dimensional characters, and anytime they get close to vulnerable work they make jokes about it and take it to the absurd instead.

The best way to take advantage of this is to start laying out the concepts of stronger scene work—finding a game, emotionally connecting, working with each other—but do it in small bites. Give them a small portion of the class where they really dig into the concepts and work on making those happen for a brief moment in the scene work. Then give them a break the rest of the time by playing the more structured and higher energy games.

As the kids in this age group have a wide difference in maturity levels, you will also get some kids who still just want to play—like in the 8-10-year-old group. When I have a mixture in a class like this, I just direct these kids differently. When we come to the deep work that they often don't really want to do, I give them slightly different challenges that will still keep them engaged, but won't ask more of them emotionally then they're able to give yet.

The Games — At this age the kids really get the games that you're teaching them. They can do some small scene work and start to make it look good and they're excited about finding the depth to the games. The scenic games mentioned before are great for this age: **Fortunately/Unfortunately, Elevator, Pan Left/Pan Right, New Choice.** And these guys can start handling more complex games like **Genre/Emotional Zones, Character Switch, Hell Dub,** and **Soap Opera.**

Once they've got a good feeling for doing these more open games, then it's fine to start introducing proto-montage formats like **Freeze** and **Character Explosion.** Have the kids play these in a way that stretches different muscles. So sometimes help them concentrate on the button—the funny moment that ends the scene. Or ask them to really watch for when a scene needs support. Or have them look for a good connection in each scene. These are good ways to play with them becoming less structured and let them take more and more responsibility for the scenes. Again, help them to keep it short and sweet, but start pushing them a little. They'll get into a pattern of how long they can go, and you want to help them extend whatever that length is to help them play longer and more interesting scenes. But you still want them to feel successful.

Social Animals — At this age the kids' brains are beginning to develop all the tools necessary to be part of a larger complex society. They're figuring out all the things they need to know to make sure they're accepted in a social sphere. The best way to support and encourage this is to play as many bonding games as possible. Games like **Untie the Knot, Traffic Cop, Norwegian Chairs, Dwarf-Wizard-Giant, Rock-Paper-Scissors Championship, Eyes on Paper,** and **Creating Shapes with Paper** are all good ways for them to practice working together in groups and figuring out how to deal with peers. Many of them will not be great at peer interaction in groups to start off with, so you'll need to stay alert to smooth over any tensions that might occur during the exercises.

This is also a brilliant time to work on the concept of taking care of your partner in the scene. Again, they're new at this so have patience! However, getting them to work together in pairs is a great way to help them support each other later in scene work. Games like the **Mirroring Game, Color/Advance, Blind Trust Walks,** and even **Yes, Let's** can be a great way of helping them figure out how to support their partner. Again, stay close as they'll need help feeling out how to help their partner and to stay on task with helping them.

Clever Kids — With this age some of the kids have figured out how to be clever, which is great. They're discovering humor and how to use it in the world. They're not only repeating jokes, they're figuring out how to make them in the first place.

The problem is that many are not very good at it yet—they use heavy-handed "rules" for humor that may only work some of the time and be just kind of obnoxious the rest of the time. Like the 8-10-year-old crowd, they figure out something that got them a laugh once and then want to do that all the time.

With these kids it's fun to start unpacking what makes something funny and it's okay to be super honest with them and say things like "Okay that bit you just did, or the joke you just told didn't really work, do you know why?" And then start working with them on how to turn their heavy-handed humor into something that's actually enjoyable for everyone. I like to tell them that I will help them be funny, but they have to trust me and let me help them do it so they'll be seen as funny instead of annoying. These guys know they're obnoxious, they just don't really know why. And often they don't care that much—if they're a little less mature, the fact that they pleased themselves and no one else with a bit is usually okay with them. However, with a little coaching, when they see that they really can get more and better laughs, then they usually come around. Not that they stop completely. These are the awesome kids who will become adults and tell dad jokes. The goal is just to make the jokes something that will more often elicit a laugh instead of an eye roll, or even punishment.

Humor — The 11-13-year-old kids as well as teens really like absurd humor, which is great—I encourage them to write lots of YouTube sketches and film them. The problem is that absurdist humor doesn't work for most improv audiences, especially when you consider that their main audiences will be their parents. Work with them on taking their awesome absurdist humor and giving it a little form and shape so it'll be easier for them to work with their partners and please their audiences.

Another thing that's similar is that the kids LOVE in-jokes. They will often do something really funny in one of the first classes and then they'll find it hilarious whenever they bring it up again. Use this to teach them about callbacks and how funny they can be. But as they get closer to the showcase, this needs to be addressed. I like to ask them how the audience will feel when they bring up something that they all find hilarious, but the audience doesn't understand at all. If you ask a question, they'll usually figure it out themselves and that saves you a lecture moment.

Transgendered Youth — This is the age that you will occasionally, if you've built a safe space, get a child who asks to be treated like a different gender than their biology indicates. In my experience, this is fine and doesn't cause problems with the class. Since kids will follow your lead on how to deal with behavior they don't understand, just tell the class that the student is now being called by this name and please refer to them by these pronouns. If the kids ask questions, just say that the child is trying this out to see if it feels right. Or if the child is very certain they're a different gender, just let the kids know that from now on we'll be using this name and pronoun. Questions are best dealt with quickly and honestly but without too much info. Just gently let the kids know that most of their questions are irrelevant to class.

Teens

Teens are basically just very new and very tender young adults. In large part their brain development is established and they will only grow what is already there. Be aware that their hormones make everything—emotions, experiences, and especially trauma—much stronger. These kids are experiencing for the first time all the feelings and emotions that you've been dealing with your entire life. So, the feelings are the same, just spiked with hormones and with no experience in how to deal with them.

The kids are also very hungry for work and meaning. They really enjoy working hard, and will want to have feedback and more nuanced discussions of why things work and don't work. They love being asked why and trying to figure it out. Step back as much as you can and let them discover things. It will make a much stronger impression if they make discoveries themselves.

Complexity — The teens can completely understand complexity, both in scenes and discussions. Your lectures can be a little longer than one to two minutes, especially if you ask their help in figuring out why a thing is true. Their characters can be more fleshed out and three-dimensional. Their scene work can have more nuanced play, with layers of meanings. And you can even start short narratives with these guys.

With teens you can discuss much more complex concepts, like the "second show," the concept that the audience is watching two shows at once—the scene you're putting on, and the second show, where the improvisers are playing together and working to put on this show. It's a pretty complex topic, but teens will understand it. Let them play with some of these more complex issues in scenes then discuss them afterwards to see what they think. In general at this age (as with adults), it's good to make a mixture of active working on things and discussion.

I've noticed an interesting dynamic with the teens. They'll be playing a scene that isn't working for whatever reason. But they will continue smiling and joking and trying to make it work, trying to push through. I call stop and ask if this is working. Their faces all drop and they look frustrated and sad. We will discuss what might help the scene, then I send them back. When they get it right, they totally know it, and after the scene is called, they will be elated and excited again. At this age, they can totally handle this rollercoaster of emotion. Just help them remember what it was that sent them on the right track, and bring up "Remember that thing you figured out?" That will help them take ownership of their learning and let them access the memory of that sweet feeling of success.

Complying — At this point behavior is not much of a problem at all. At most you will have a problem with them talking too much in class, but for the most part if you ask them to do something, they will probably do it. You don't even have as much a problem with status and treating the odd kids differently.

Genders — As they mature teens will start working with the other gender. Friendships across gender lines develop, and you can have a class of primarily one gender and the other one won't be as uncomfortable.

Please never tease younger teens about romantic feelings—these are very new and fresh and they just don't have the experience to be able to laugh at themselves yet; the stakes are too high for that. Instead just assume that every friendship is just that, a friendship, and treat it as you would any friendship.

Many of the kids will also begin to be fine playing a game where they take on the identity of another gender. Not every kid—often more conservative boys will have a hard time playing girls, but gently play around with that. Don't push the kids too far past their comfort zone, but go ahead and work on cross-gender play some. It's good for kids to be able to play whatever character comes up in a scene and not worry about their own identity as a stumbling block. Also, it gives them some insight and compassion to play different roles in life.

Romantic Scenes — Try to be sensitive in your use of romantic scenes. This age can handle being an old married couple, or a mother and father dealing with a child. However, first date scenes or ones that have a high amount of romance in them, are a little intense for these guys. I'm not saying you shouldn't do it—you could and maybe should, depending on your comfort level—but expect a lot of giggling and bailing emotionally, because this is something they're dealing with in real life and it can be really scary. It's safer to do these scenes in class, and not make them play out a first date in front of their parents in the showcase. Talk about awkward!

CHAPTER EIGHT

ZOOM! TEACHING IMPROV ONLINE

Like most people I was bopping along enjoying teaching in-person improv classes when Whoosh! Everything shut down during the 2020 pandemic, and people were not allowed to meet in groups and certainly not indoors. Fortunately for me this coincided with Spring Break. I took a week to figure out how to change my classes based on connection and interaction into classes that could work online.

I will not say that those first classes were stellar successes, but fortunately knowing how both kids and improv work, I was able to adjust. Over the course of a few months, I developed a strong sense of how to teach improv to children online.

Of course, in the future beyond the publication of this book, we'll be able to meet again in person, but still I've found that there are some nice advantages to teaching online and wanted to share those with you. The most obvious is that you're able to have kids from all over the country take your classes. I love the classes that have at least one person from each US time zone in them.

Teaching online also means that parents don't have to fight traffic or find parking to reach your class.

I personally think I will continue to have at least a class or two online even when it's no longer required.

Compassion

The first absolutely most important thing about teaching online is to have compassion. On the most basic level, the technology can be very trying.

The kids will have slow internet connections. Or else they'll be on a phone or tablet that doesn't show the class as well. Or maybe they'll be in a car taking the class while the parents drive who knows where. These things are frustrating but not impossible to deal with. Slow down. Take a deep breath. And do whatever you can to help the kids (or yourself) through the technical difficulties. Often, because they have been in a similar situation, the other kids will have an answer about how to deal with issues. They like to use their knowledge to help out their classmates, which is a great way to build some trust. That's kind of beautiful when it happens.

During times of crisis like the one in which I write this book, it's important to be aware that the children might be having troubles in their personal lives. The world is a crazy place when you're forced to move from real life to virtual to meet most of your socialization and educational needs. Kids are generally resilient, but that doesn't mean they don't need to process what is happening in the world around them. Be aware that some of their behaviors might get more difficult, and they may regress. Specifically, children might be acting about 2-3 years younger than their current age. This is a typical response to trauma and uncertainty. Again, take a deep breath and slow down. Try to see this for what it's—the kids are dealing with something that everyone is having a hard time with. Realize that you will be one of the few adults in their lives and if you can model being kind and patient with difficulties, you're teaching them a very important lesson.

And of course, have compassion for yourself. In the beginning I found teaching online to be very frustrating and draining. I had to give myself the time to adjust to the situation rather than just push myself to my limit. I found several strategies that helped me be the best teacher I could be and maintain my healthy and positive teacher composure.

One thing that will really help you teach online—as it helps in real life—is setting up a classroom that will lead to success. Even though you're in a virtual space and have much less control over the children's environments, you still have dominion over your space.

Set Up the Classroom for Success

Pick times and days that will be supportive to the kids. I have noticed that in the online world, everyone sleeps much later. Starting classes at 9:30 meant that many kids would not join. Even in my 10:30 class I'd have sleepy-faced kids with bedhead tuning in while still under the blankets. So consider having the classes later in the day.

It's hard these days to know when school is, but if you have classes on weekdays try to have some time between the end of school and the start of your classes. The amount of screen time kids are consuming in the online environment is huge, so it's best to have some downtime/snack-time/run-around time for the kids before your program starts.

When the parents sign up, it's great if you can send them either an automatic confirmation or an email letting them know how to sign on to your virtual class platform. In that email, you can also give tips for making the classroom more successful. I found that only about 50% of parents followed those tips, but it can be helpful at least for those parents.

Let the parents know:

1. How to sign in
2. What kind of set up they will need (laptop, tablet, etc.)
3. If possible, to have the child in a room by themselves
4. If possible, to limit outside distractions such as food
5. If they have more than one child in the household taking the class, then have them on separate screens
6. Have the child in a place where they can get up and move around

If you start out with these suggestions, you're seeding a successful environment for your kiddos.

And you? You also need to have a good environment to make sure you can show up in the best possible way for the kids. When I first started out teaching online, I just stacked furniture on my bed and put my computer on top of it. While that technically works, there were issues like worrying about my leaning stack of furniture, boxes, and books tumbling down. I eventually got a desk that has an adjustable height to put my laptop on, and that works much better.

If possible, set yourself up in a place where you can stand and move around. It's possible to teach sitting down, but you lose a lot of energy that way. When you stand, you have the ability to show the games fully and at full range. It makes a difference.

Before the class begins, you should certainly get to know the online service you're using. Set up a practice run, preferably with other people so you can see how things work, and your assistants, if you're lucky enough to have any, can give you feedback about how it looks on their end.

If possible, make sure you have a desk or writing space so that you can take notes during the class. I like to have the kids' names written down so that I can more easily refer to them. They do love to rename themselves in their Zoom boxes, so having their actual names can be helpful, especially with a new group of kids.

What the kids see behind you is also important. I am fortunate that I can face a nice bright window and my background is just a wall and door. I want to make sure I don't have anything interesting in my background because the kids will notice and be distracted. If you can't create a blank space then think about getting a curtain you can hang. As a last resort, a virtual background can be helpful. For all of us who have spent far too much time on Zoom this year, you know a virtual background is a last resort because often the service will confuse parts of you with the background and you will "lose" pieces of yourself. This can make explaining games very difficult, and it can look just downright creepy!

Now I have a nice desk with two plants, a notebook, my pencil, a drink, and my computer. Everything is set up just so. I have everything at hand and don't have to go looking for anything that I need. This makes it much easier for me to be present. I suggest that you take some time to think about what environment will support you to be present and available.

Setting the Kids Up for Success

Start the "meeting" about 5-10 minutes before the actual class time. Make it so that the kids will remain in the "waiting room." This means the kids can come on at any time before the class and know that they're in the right place and that the class will start soon. And you can make sure everything is ready before you let them in.

I suggest you start letting the kids in about 3 minutes before the start of the class. This way you get to greet kids early and see how they're doing. Write down their names as they come in and number them according to who comes in first. Then "rename" each child and put their number before their name. This way when you play "circle" games the kids will know the order. This makes the rest of class much easier. I know it seems tiny, but the kids are more likely to be on time if they're given a lower number when they show up early. It just goes to show how even the smallest positive motivations can be super helpful. I even stopped numbering myself so that the first lucky child could have the number 1.

Start these classes by letting the kids know what is happening. Being online, at least initially, is unsettling enough that the kids need to have a little stability. Letting them know what is coming is a good way of giving the kids a bit of solid footing.

Give them a layout of how the class will work. Such as "we'll start with some warm-up games, then do some games that teach the theme for today and finally we'll end with some games that you might play in an actual show."

Give the kids any important instructions about space upfront. That way they know what is okay and what is not.

If a kid has a virtual background, find a way to let them know that's okay at least for now. Kids love their virtual backgrounds and get sad if they can't show the other kids their skills and pictures. However, there are some games where it just doesn't work. And some pictures that are just distracting. Let them know right off the bat what your boundaries are. Something like, "I love that bunny picture! I'm fine with virtual backgrounds, but if they're distracting then we might have to stop them. And there are some games that just don't work with virtual backgrounds, but I'll let you know when we get to those." This lets them know that you appreciate their efforts and are willing to work with them. I have found even the most distractible children to be willing to work with you if you're willing to work with them.

For the chat function, just ignore it unless it becomes a problem. The kids love making friends and saying things in the chat can be helpful with that. However, I noticed that some kids would start sending pictures and links to games and weird strings of characters in the chat. If this happens it does become distracting, so you'll want to give the kids a chance or two to keep it under control. Tell them what the problem is and how it's affecting class and ask them to stop. If they can't stop, change your permissions so that they can only chat with you. You still need to have the chat function for yourself so the kids can message you privately if they need anything.

If one of the kids has a very noisy environment, ask them to move if possible and if it's not possible, ask them to stay on mute whenever they're not talking. If they're unable to follow that, you can mute them from your controls. The background noise can make it very difficult for the other children to focus. Fortunately, the kids are often already aware of this and will be willing to work with you. Most of the time, they also don't enjoy the distractions.

Tools You Can Use

During the class, there are several functions in virtual classrooms that can be very helpful. I love using breakout rooms. This is a perfect function to give the kids extra time and space to play a game or do an exercise. Start out by showing the game to the entire group and make sure they understand the instructions. After you send them to the rooms, join each room one at a time to make sure they understand what they're supposed to be doing and don't have any questions. I can never tell how long is long enough, so I set a timer for the minutes that I think they'll need. Then when I think the time should be over, I send a message asking them to "wrap up and come back" when they're finished. This will get them coming back at different times, but that allows me to check in and see how they enjoyed the games. It gives them a little extra attention as well. When I send the kids to breakout rooms, I tell them that if they don't want to play the games, it's okay to just hang out and talk while they're in the rooms. Connection can be just as important, if not more so than whatever game you're teaching. I love it when I bring the kids back and they're laughing as they come on screen!

I use the chat function for games such as **Hesitation Debate.** The students who are not participating in the debate can send their words via the chat, which is super fun.

The chat can also be used for private messages, like when a child would like to talk to you, but is uncomfortable talking publicly. Or when you have to ask a child to stop something, but don't want to do that in front of everyone. The chat gives you a little bit of privacy.

The chat can also be very useful as a sort of blackboard. I put the "story spine" in the chat so that everyone can see it as they take their turns. This makes it easier to see, and everyone knows what is happening.

There is also a function in most of the virtual meeting software that will allow you to "share screens." This can be a super fun function. One of the screens is a place where you can draw. This allows you to illustrate things and acts as sort of a blackboard. I love it for showing what the structure of a scene looks like.

This function is also great for making pictures together. I had one group of kids who loved this more than anything and would happily work together drawing things and adding to each other's art. The results were adorable, if somewhat cluttered. When you do things like this, you can take a screenshot and send it to the kids or email it to the parents. That way the kids get to "keep" their pictures.

And finally, you can share video clips—this is a fun way to find and show games. If you look up most games, there will likely be a video clip of someone playing that game on YouTube. Please, please, please review any video clips before you show them in class. Even the best ones can have inappropriate subject matter or jokes. But watching something like this together can help the kids see how a game is played and make it easier for them to understand.

Finally, at the end of class you'll want a nice way to wrap up. I really enjoy putting on some music and having each of the kids lead us in dance. It's super high energy and I love the dance moves. However, sometimes you'll get a group that's just not into this. For these friends, try to end with the same game every time. Having repetition builds some security into the class. My favorite is ending with **Word at a Time Saying**—we just go around in a circle until everyone has gone at least once.

Distractions

In most virtual classes, something will happen to distract the kids. A pet will walk in, or they'll see their favorite toy, or they'll want to share a picture that they found. In real life I'm more likely to keep things on a roll and keep everyone focused. In the virtual world I've found trying to keep focus just doesn't work. You're not in control of the environment, and you can't make the distractions go away. Spending a moment on the dog that walked in or the toy or the what-have-you will actually diffuse the interest in that object. Think of it like a tea kettle—the pressure is building up and if you just ignore it the distraction becomes more and more distracting. If you give the distraction a moment of attention, it's like turning off the heat. The distraction goes away and the child feels acknowledged.

One of the most distracting things actually comes from the parents. Often a well-meaning parent will come into the child's space with a plate of food. Sometimes this is just a snack and it's fine. The child might eat a couple of things but then be done. But at other times it's clearly breakfast or lunch. The child takes huge bites and plows through the food methodically. Every time you ask them to participate in class, they either show you a mouth full of "seefood" or you have to wait while they laboriously chew their fodder. As annoying as this is, there really isn't much to be done. You can try to time the bites so that you don't catch them with a full mouth, or just wait to call on them until they're done. Often the food is distracting enough that they really are not paying attention anyway.

Use the Environment

One of the nice things about virtual classes is that the kids can use all sorts of things from their own house. I love setting up a costume show—give the kids three minutes to go get a costume together and then show it. After that, use those characters in a game like **Town Hall** or **Character Advice**. They can also use stuffed animals as puppets. When a child is distracted by a stuffed animal in their room, ask them to use the animal as the character in the next scene. Or you can ask the animal questions and have the child respond for it. That is not only super validating, it's also pretty adorable and still teaches valuable improv skills.

Games in the Virtual Space

When we first jumped into the virtual space, I was sure it wouldn't work because I couldn't imagine how the games could be played through a computer screen. But then I looked at my actual syllabus and I realized that many of the games would translate quite well.

Some games like **Alien Translator** need no modification whatsoever. They don't depend on space or order to work well.

Games like **Zip Zap Zop** work with a little modification. I have the kids say the name of the person they're sending it to. This adds an extra layer to the game, but it's not terrible. **Category Die** is the same, and the kids actually are more successful with listing things—I think because having their name called is less pressure than being pointed at.

Then there are other things that don't work at all—anything that requires chanting or simultaneous action is much harder to make work.

As you choose an online game, try to think about the elements that are important to it. For example, **Kitty Cat Careers** is less fun, but still workable. Instead of chanting "Kitty Cat Careers," you can just have them clap while you chant. The kids love "cheating" with this game and bringing in props from their room or desk to help them show the career they're acting out.

Sometimes the kids ask for a specific game that they used to enjoy in real life. At first I shied away from these because I couldn't figure them out. Then I hit on a genius plan—ask the kids how it would work. The kids are super creative and often come up with really smart and workable ideas. Even if they don't, going through the process of brainstorming and then trying something out is very validating to the kids and helps them realize that they have agency in their world.

The other delightful thing that came out of this process was developing new games with the kids. Maybe I'd have the germ of an idea, or we'd start with a game that doesn't quite work and then the kids and I would brainstorm and try different things until we came up with something totally new. Not only does this give you a nice new game, but it also gives the kids practice in the process of creating things. Everybody wins!

Virtual Showcases

For some reason, I've found that the kids don't seem to need to show their skills off as much in the virtual world. Some classes I ran had no showcases and the kids didn't seem to miss them at all. Other classes did have showcases, but the kids just didn't seem to get as excited about them. I wonder if it's because being on a screen already feels performative.

However, showcases are still fun and it's a nice way to cap off a class. More of the kid's family can drop in since this is in a virtual world where space doesn't matter as much. Often even office workers can take a short break to watch their favorite young relative's showcase.

At the Hideout we perform in Zoom, and stream to Twitch—a live streaming service. However, Facebook Live will also work, as will many other options. The webinar function in Zoom can be great for showcases. Have the kids be panelists. Zoom automatically creates an audience by keeping the guests muted and their cameras off.

The first thing to keep in mind for a showcase is to set the kids up for success, which of course you'd do in an in-person showcase as well. For a virtual showcase though, you want to make sure they look great on the screen. Pick games that the kids already do really well at and practice those. You want to showcase each child at least a little bit so that they can feel like they've really done something. In an in-person showcase I might throw a new game at the kids to see the spark and spontaneity, but this is not a good idea online, as there's no support from the audience to act as feedback and let the kids know they're doing fine.

Speaking of feedback, consider asking all the children to keep their microphones live. That way the kids on screen can hear the laughter and reactions from the kids who are watching. That can be very helpful feedback for the children who are performing.

These showcases should be very short. Because of the lack of feedback, they can be very draining for the kids. They tend to hit their limit well before they would in an in-person showcase. I find that 15-20 minutes is just fine for elementary age kids, and 20-30 is good for the middle school and high school kids.

You'll still want to get input from the audience. In most streaming services, there is a chat function. However, often there is a15-ish second lag between what you do and what the audience sees. This can feel like forever to wait for a response, so it's best to ask for a suggestion first and then describe or set up the game. For example, if I was setting up **Alien Translator,** I would start like this:

> "Oh, that last game was great! Thank you! Audience, we're going to need a planet that someone might come from—made up or real—and some questions that you might like to ask an alien. Even after we start, you can still send in more questions. Okay for this game I'll need X to be the host, then I'll need Y to be the translator and finally Z will be our Alien. Everyone else can you please keep your cameras off? Thank you. And it looks like in the chat, the suggestion of the planet is: Freon! Excellent! Kids, you may begin!"

This gives the audience time to respond without waiting through downtime.

You'll need to coach the parents on how to respond. That way they know what is acceptable. Let the parents know that their responses in chat are super important and help the show go along well. Then after each game say something like, "Give them a cheer or an emoji in the chat!"

The children can't see it during the show, but it does keep the audience engaged. Also, many of the children will watch themselves later and the chat will show up as the recording goes so they can see how the audience responded to them.

Virtual improv classes are intimidating at first, but with a little adjustment they can still be a fun and valuable part of your students' lives.

CHAPTER NINE

WHAT WENT WRONG? THE CHALLENGES

Let me be completely honest with you—nothing ever goes totally smoothly. Some classes have a harder time getting a specific skill than others. Some kids have a harder time behaving during class. And sometimes the class just feels like it doesn't work. There are correctives for certain improv problems, just as there are for certain behaviors. It's always best to assume that every child is doing their best and mistakes and misbehaviors are just part of their learning process. With that in mind, here are several ways to address challenges that might arise in class.

Common Improv Problems and Exercises for Correcting Them

1. **Negativity** — Negativity is starting a scene or game being combative, sad, angry, or otherwise negative. It is a standard way for improvisers of all ages to keep themselves safe and avoid vulnerability. It also will frequently get a laugh. The problem is that it only really gets a laugh as it destroys the scene, leaving nowhere else to go, and alienating the audience. I've noticed that for some kids, being negative is often their only control in the world, so they use it as a way to gain power. The problem is, it's like holding the ball in basketball—once you've got it, you really can't do anything with it and the game or scene has to end. It's better to start positive and then let the scene/game develop—even if it turns negative appropriately, it will carry more weight and meaning. Kids of all ages can be coached to be more positive. Our catchphrase is "Happy, Healthy, Friendly."

Correctives — Play scenes where every time they do something happy, healthy, or friendly, you ring a bell for positive reinforcement. This works for all ages. The younger kids should tell stories rather than play scenes.

For age 8 and above, play **Fortunately/Unfortunately** and put the student that has a hard time with being positive in the Fortunately spot. You can also play **I Am a Tree, Sound Ball,** and **Evolution** as a warm-up.

For middle school and teens, tell a story one sentence at a time, where each next sentence starts with the words, "Not only that!"

For all ages, **Eyes on Paper** works well. Draw two dots for eyes. The kids are in pairs and each pair has one paper with eyes. Each child has a different colored marker. They take turns drawing one portion of the face at a time, they can't cross anything out, they can only add. At the end (if they can write), they name the face by alternating writing one letter at a time.

2. **Not Adding** — This is common with certain improvisers of all ages. They will agree to anything, but they have a hard time adding information to the scene. They will often say they just can't think of anything to add. Don't worry about this for kids under the age of 8. For many of them, this is just a skill that comes later.

Correctives — For little kids, play **Please the Crown.**

For 8 and above play **Five Things**. Get them to list five things in a certain category—they don't have to be right, they just have to say five things quickly. Or try **Waiter**, where one child is the waiter and another child keeps asking questions about the menu. Clap enthusiastically when the child is able to tell about the food.

For middle school and teens, try **Hype Man**. Put a child in a scene with someone else, but give them a "hype man." Every time the child says anything, the hype man affirms it and enthusiastically supports the offer. **One-Minute Monologue** also works well. Have them face a wall somewhere a little away from anyone else. Set a timer for 1 minute, give them a thing to talk about, and let them go. You can stretch this up to 5 minutes (for advanced teens). If they're having trouble coming up with what to talk about, have them explore the history of the subject or character, the philosophy of the character, or give a metaphor and say, "It's just like...."

For all ages, I recommend **Commercials**. Set up a specific area of the stage, with all the children off to the side in a line. When you ring a bell, the kids come out one at a time and perform a commercial, or tv show, or whatever. When you ring the bell again, the child leaves and the next one comes out. Keep them short—5 or 10 seconds is fine—but let any hesitant kids go a little longer than they might feel comfortable, and slowly help them go on longer and longer.

3. **Hesitating** — The hesitant child is the one that doesn't come out in line games, that has a hard time getting on stage, and who seems to fade back in the energy of the class. The thing is, when this child does come out, they usually have good stuff to add to the scene. Often their hesitation is just because they have a shyer personality and will need some space to jump out and join. Ultimately this child needs affirmations that they belong and they're welcome on the stage and that we want to have their participation.

   You'll also want to make sure this child doesn't get bulldozed by some of the louder kids, and you can work with them together to help balance each other out.

   This tends to be more of a problem in the middle school and teen classes.

   Correctives — In line games, call the children out by name, or have them go in order. This way the hesitant child will become more confident in their scenes. Don't make this child go first—they need to watch a little to feel brave enough.

   For games like **I Am a Tree**, where the kids just jump in when they're inspired, take a different strategy. I ask the kids to notice how many other kids there are and then figure out how often they should jump out. If they're jumping out too much, then when they feel inspired, ask them to pick a hesitant classmate and encourage them to jump out.

   Break up into small groups and pairs frequently—often the hesitant child will gain confidence from having some success in small groups where the pressure is lower.

4. **Stage Hogs** — These boisterous kids are the awesome ones who love to be on stage so much that they don't really notice that they're taking up all the stage time! They're simply very enthusiastic and have not yet built their ability to see what others need. You don't want to dampen their excitement for the stage, but rather, just help them learn a little empathy for the other kids who also want to play.

   For the kids under 8, don't worry about this too much, just go in order most of the time to make sure everyone gets a chance. It takes a while for this age to develop this type of empathy.

   For the older kids you'll want to follow much of the same advice as for the hesitant child. Going in order, asking them to look at the numbers in the class, carefully pairing them in games and scenes to give them other kids who will match their energy, and having them work on giving space to more hesitant kids—all these strategies should work.

   Correctives — Play a scene where the boisterous child can only say "yeah," "sure," or "I'll go along with that."

   In any scene or game have your boisterous kid take a breath, count to 5 in their head, or repeat the last line in their head, before they can respond.

   Play **Ball**. Try to keep a ball in the air by hitting it one child at a time, counting every time someone hits it—when it touches the floor, you have to start over. In this game, kids who are dominant will soon see that by leaving their part of the circle and coming to the middle they make it more likely the ball will fall behind them. From time to time, have the kids break into small groups and brainstorm 3 things that will make the game work better. This will have them working with their peers and they will hear that their domination of the game is frustrating for everyone else and messes up the game.

5. **Blocking and Bulldozing** — Blocking is when a child refuses to accept the offer of another child. Bulldozing is when they take over the scene and don't let the other improvisor have input. This is not fun for the scene partner, and often keeps the scene from going forward or makes it hard to justify what just happened.

   The little kids do this a lot, but it's something that happens at every level.

Correctives — For little kids, play **Eyes on Paper**. Have one child tell a story and the other act it out. Rotate the narrator. This is a variation on **Typewriter.**

For 8 and above play **Hype Man**, with the scene blocker in the hype man position. Another idea for this age group is have the blocker repeat the last line out loud before they can respond. For example, Child A says, "I'm going to the store." The blocking child says, "You're going to the store. I'm going to go with you."

For teens, have them make strong eye contact with their partner in the scene. They can also repeat the last line in their head before they respond.

For all ages, do three line scene starts and every response must start with "Yes, and."

7. **Negotiating/Transactions** — Negotiating is where the child says "yes," but then puts conditions on it. For example, Child A says, "Let's go fight that dragon." The negotiating child says, "Yes, but I get the good armor." This stops the forward momentum of the scene. Transactions are literally scenes where the kids play out buying something. Middle school and young high school students will play these out over and over again. I think they like these so much because these are one of the few interactions that kids have with strangers, so they know how it will play out and don't have to worry about making anything up. Although you will see these in younger children, you don't need to address them until they get to middle school and above.

Correctives — When they get into a negotiation have a narrator character say, "Later at the dragon's cave." Or "meanwhile," or anything that will move the plot forward. After they've experienced this move a few times, they'll get better at moving the plot along on their own.

Play **Slo Motion Samurai** a few times. Let them know that the battles are negotiations and that the point is to end them and move on. In this game you should always be striving for glorious death rather than victory.

Play scenes where they're doing space work—whittling, washing dishes, weeding, etc.—but the rule is, you can't talk about what you're doing at all.

Play **Musical Eye Contact**. Even if they get into a transaction scene, they'll be so connected that it will have the depth and relationship the scene needs.

8. **Bailing** — Bailing is when a child is engaged in a scene, then doesn't know what to do or say next. Their typical reactions? They usually fall down, or run around in circles, or flap their hands, all while yelling chaotic and indistinguishable noises! Older children do something similar by making a joke that will undercut the scene, or creating something completely out of the blue or unrelated to the scene, or literally just walking off stage. This isn't a problem you can completely fix, but you can make it so that the kids go longer before they bail.

   Correctives — Anything that slows the children down will usually work here. Have them count to 5 before responding. Or repeat the last line they heard in their head before responding. You can also have them respond by repeating the last offer out loud. And, a corrective that also works on stage is taking a breath before speaking. All of these will give the child a little time to think and give them a chance to figure out what the next beat is.

   The other way to approach this problem is with connection, especially for the high school kids. Games such as **Touch Talk, Musical Eye Contact, Soap Opera,** and other scenes where they're touching each other the whole time will give them some organization around the awkward intimacy and help them play through.

Common Behavioral Problems and Ways to Correct Them

1. **The Kid Who Can't Stop Talking** — This child may be otherwise well-behaved and pretty smart, but they just can't stop talking no matter how many times you correct them. They don't want to be out of line, but they just can't help themselves. Often this will be in the form of quips after you say something. These are often clever and funny and you don't want to stifle them. Instead I let them know that for most teachers they'll let the first quip go and maybe even smile at it, the second quip will push it for them, and they'll always come down on the third quip. So, I tell them, if you're going to do the third, it better

be worth it to you! This is a fun way to acknowledge their playfulness and let them know the limits of it.

However, there are also kids who will talk to their neighbors when you're trying to talk, which means neither one of the kids will have heard what you were saying. For these kids, there are a few strategies.

Correctives — First of all, try to make sure the kids have some time for social talk. If they don't show up early enough for this, make little breaks in the exercises so that they can have a minute to talk first.

If that doesn't work, separate the talker from their favorite talking partners. Or encourage the other children to put a finger to their lips when the talker is talking to them. Or put them next to you or to your assistant.

It is likely that no matter what you do, the child will still have a hard time not talking. So just repeat where you need to, correct as often as you feel necessary, but try not to make them feel too bad about it as we want them to enjoy their time in class.

2. **The Shy Kid** — There are two versions of this. The truly shy kids would like to be on stage and engage with the other kids, but are just terrified. Then there is the child who has learned to get attention through acting shy. Fortunately, you handle them both pretty much the same way.

Correctives — Let them watch instead of participating. Make sure they're sitting alone, but it's okay for them to just watch. You should make occasional offers for them to join, but not so much that it detracts from what you're doing, or gives a lot of attention to the child.

Give them more time to answer. Smile and make eye contact if possible and wait patiently for them to be able to engage.

Work in pairs or small groups, pairing the shy kid with partners who will be supportive but won't bulldoze them.

For the showcases, allow them to choose how much they want to be in. If they don't want to do anything then see if they're interested in doing tech instead, or in sitting next to you and helping you keep track of the games.

These kids will often be shy until they feel comfortable and safe in the class, so your main goal is to give them the time and space to develop that trust.

3. **The Kid No One Likes** — Unfortunately, there may be times where you've got a child that no one really likes. They may be different in some way that stands out, or they may have off-putting behaviors.

   Correctives — The kids will follow your lead on how you treat this child, so try to have an extra dose of patience. Be firm and kind and remember to keep in mind that every child has a place and a story. Eventually, some of the hardest kids to deal with end up being really talented adults.

   In classes where we have kids who are not readily liked or accepted by others, we play a lot of bonding games. **Untying the Knot, Trust Falls, Blind Trust Walks, I'm Cool and So Are You** or **Come Over Here If** are all good bonding games that will help bring the class together.

   Be aware of which kids in particular have a strong reaction against certain kids that may be hard to like, and steer clear of partnering them together, especially if there have already been issues that day. Try to rotate this kid through the different groups so that one tolerant or sensitive child doesn't always have to partner with them, and so the other kids start to learn that this kid does have good qualities (you may need to highlight and really reinforce those).

4. **The Mischievous Leader** — This child is playful, intelligent, and a born leader. They will figure out ways to cause chaos in the classroom and bring other children along with them. Although you want to encourage a certain amount of mischievousness, you also obviously need to have the kids follow you so that you can teach the class.

   Correctives — Often this child has not bought into the program or improv in general. You may need to work on engaging them in positive ways. Ask them to help you demonstrate the game or exercise you're setting up.

   When they make a good point, be sure to call them by name and repeat the point.

Frequently call on them first.

Ask them to help with another child—for example if a child comes in late, have the leader explain what's going on to the newly arrived child.

Co-opt any rebellions. For example, if the kids all start doing some gesture or word, join in and do it with them. Push this as far as it will go. Hopefully this will end in laughter and fun and you can explain the lesson from it as if you were wanting to do that all along.

For kids in middle school and above, find a reason to leave the classroom for about 30 seconds. Before you leave, put the leader child in charge. When you come back, thank them for keeping the classroom orderly. Or engage in whatever mischief they've come up with. Frequently it will be hiding. Make a fun game out of not being able to find them at all.

If you can sufficiently engage this child, you can convert them into a positive leader in the class who may end up being a big help to you!

5. **The Kid Who Challenges Your Authority** — These kids are the one who ask why they have to do something and frequently say that the games are dumb. Often the other kids will be ambivalent towards them, but it's still hard for them to be joyfully creative about what they're doing if someone has just labeled it "dumb."

   The challenger is often a child who doesn't want to be there. Maybe their parents made them do this, or there's something else they really enjoy that they'd rather be doing, or it could be that they're experiencing trauma somewhere in their lives and letting go and trusting other people is just too much for them to handle emotionally.

   Correctives — Allow this child to sit out of any game they don't want to do. If other children want to sit out too, this is fine, but they have to sit alone and not talk to one another. When they get bored, they'll realize that playing games is more fun than sitting out.

   If you think they will respond well, ask them to help out by leading games, or helping you demo it.

   If it keeps going, sit down with the child and ask them if they like the class. Don't be insulted if they don't—they might not.

Then ask why they're coming to the class. Listen carefully for any clues that might help you engage them. Then, invite them to brainstorm ways to make the class more fun, while not messing it up for the other children who may already be having fun. If you listen and engage, they will often start to work with you. Again, these children can end up being really valuable members of class once they feel fully engaged.

6. **Offensive Content** — This includes swearing, references to drugs, sex, and violence, and offensive stereotypes. As we encourage the kids to be open and say the first thing that comes out of their mouth, this is bound to come up from time to time.

   Correctives — If it seems like it's truly a slip-up, don't make a big deal about it, but don't let it go either or else all the other kids will start playing with "slipping up."

   If you've played **New Choice** before, you can simply say, "Whoops! New choice." You can laugh about it with the kids, but keep it going so that it doesn't become a big issue.

   If it looks intentional, then a neutral "We don't say that word in here" works well. And then move on to the next thing. Try to remove all the judgment from your voice, and just let them know calmly what the boundaries in the class are.

   As the children get older, they will start playing with themes of sex, drugs, and graphic violence. In a way, this is actually good because they're acting out the themes of their lives and processing things they've heard or seen elsewhere. But you must have a sense of how far is too far. Again, you don't want to be judgmental about things, but you do want to be clear. Feel free to blame the parents, saying something like "You know your parents would kill me if I let you get away with that." You can also point out that some of these topics will be alienating to a family audience, which is who they'll be playing to eventually. Or just say that you're uncomfortable with them exploring these themes in class.

   If what they're doing or saying becomes truly offensive or hurtful to someone in class, then you need to stop and address it. A discussion about why something is offensive or how it made the other person feel is very important. It's very unlikely that the offending child wants to be offensive—they're probably just unaware of what effect their words have or else they're copying something they heard and laughed at elsewhere. Teens tend to be defensive about this type of thing, so handle it as lightly as possible, while still making sure they understand the boundary.

Most of the teens will already be on board with a lot of social justice issues, so discussions of race and gender and class politics can actually go really well. The thing you'll want to watch for is that you don't shame someone. For example, if a kid says something about a marginalized race or ethnicity, often the other kids will jump on him and use sarcasm or judgmental language to correct him. You'll want to remind the kids that we're all just learning, and that supporting your partner means helping them see what might be offensive without shaming them.

A child who's been the subject of one of these comments or jokes will often try to play it off. They might insist that they're not hurt by the comment and that it's just funny. You don't ever want to ask this child to explain how a comment like this felt to them—that's a lot of pressure after having just been confronted with an objectionable comment. Instead, jump in and put it on yourself. Say that you're uncomfortable with this or that it offends you. And if the child who is the subject of the comments insists that they don't mind, go ahead and point out that they're not the only person of their race, gender, etc. and that we need to be respectful of all people, even if they're not in the room. Remind them that they may be in the audience someday.

CHAPTER TEN

YOUR REAL CLIENTS? THE PARENTS

When I first started teaching, most of the parents in my program were friends or friends of friends. This was great in some ways—these people already trusted me and knew that I was going to take good care of their children. However, it also set up boundary problems, such as parents who wanted me to change the class structure to accommodate their child; parents who were late; parents who would tell me about a cute play they had seen and ask if we could do that for the showcase. But also, parents who were always confused about when classes were and when the showcase was and what they needed to do when. I realized that the answer to all of these problems was me providing a lot more structure and oversharing information as often as possible.

Parents can be wonderfully kind, supportive, and become advocates for your program, or they can cause all sorts of problems and be a real headache. This chapter will show you ways to keep most of your parents in the first category.

Registration

The parents may be excited—they're signing their child up for a new program, one they certainly didn't take as a child. It's interesting and different and just slightly scary. You can help them set expectations by keeping the registration process as normal and easy as possible.

Start off on the right foot by getting all the info you need right up front. If you're taking phone registrations this is easy—just ask them! If you're doing online sign-ups then try to manage it so that they will give the basic registration info when they sign up. If your system doesn't work that way, then you'll need to ask for that in the first email you send.

The information that you'll need for classes will be:

Parent's Name
Parent's Email
Parent's Phone Number
Child's Name
Child's Date of Birth
Any Special Needs

With the parent's phone and email info, you'll be able to communicate quickly and effectively with them. Email is preferable for regular communications, but it's good to have the phone number in case of an emergency, or if you just need to text them something quickly. When you do talk to them on the phone, leave time to have a good conversation. A friendly conversation will go a long way to making sure the parents are happy with you and the program.

Make sure to get the child's date of birth rather than the age. In my experience, parents will sometimes exaggerate their child's age (because they assume their child is particularly advanced!), but they won't change the date of birth. If you have the date of birth, you'll be able to track their age through the years, assuming they stay in your program.

Make sure to ask about special needs. This leaves it open for the parents to communicate any of their fears or concerns. The parent of a special needs child may let you know about their child's needs here and maybe even strategies. This way you can follow up and get the information you need before the first day of class. If what they write seems especially complicated, then you might want to call them to discuss their child directly.

Email Communication

Often your first contact with the parents will be the confirmation letter you send to them when they sign up. If you send this to them shortly after they sign up, they will know they're registered and ready to go. This will eliminate some of their worry about the class and your program. It also shows that you're a professional and that you have the program well in hand.

This is the typical confirmation letter I send:

> Dear Parents:
>
> Thank you so much for signing your child up to take improv classes at the Hideout Theatre.
>
> Your child's class will be on Saturdays, January 21st - May 13th, 10:00 am-11:00 am. We will skip March 11th and 18th for spring break. Our showcase will be on May 6th from 2:00 pm-3:30 pm.
>
> Your teacher will be *Teacher McTeacher.*
>
> We will send you a Welcome Letter on the Friday before class starts so you have all the info for parking and such.
>
> Please let me know if you have any questions.
>
> Thank you!

After that I will send a Welcome Letter the day before class starts. This serves as a reminder that class will begin the next day. Believe it or not, parents do forget sometimes. In this letter I give them all the basic information they need for the class. This will preemptively answer a lot of their questions, and reassure them again that you're a competent child-care provider who will take care of their children and communicate well with them as parents.

Here is a typical Welcome Letter I send:

> Hi y'all,
>
> Improv class starts tomorrow and we're all very excited to meet new students and see returning students again!
>
> Your instructor will be *Teacher McTeacher* and your TA will be *Assistant O'Assistant* who are cc'd on the email here. The teacher's phone

number is *123-4567*. Please text or email them if you're going to miss or be late to a class. If you have general questions about the class, you can email me directly.

This semester we'll be in the upstairs theater. Go through the coffee shop and past the restrooms. There will be a staircase on your left—come on upstairs and the theater will be in front of you.

Tomorrow I will be in the coffee shop to check your child in and make sure they get to the right place.

Parking is always tricky downtown. If you can find public transportation, awesome! If not, then you can look for street parking along Brazos, 8th, Guadalupe, and 7th streets. The meters are $1.30 an hour and they take credit cards.

Please have the kids wear comfortable clothes they can move in and shoes that won't come off their feet when they're playing.

Please let me know if you have any questions. I am best reached by email.

Thank you and I look forward to seeing you all tomorrow!

Phone Communication

If a child is new to the program, often the parents will call you. It may be that they really just need to talk with someone in the program, to hear your voice and be reassured that you're real and competent. They might be asking questions that are common sense or that they could easily find out on the website. Just be patient with this and talk to them for a bit. Your job here is to reassure them that everything will be fine, and you do this by answering their questions patiently and thoroughly. Some parents will want to chat for a long time, possibly veering off into talking about their lives or "kids these days." Sometimes it gets frustrating, especially if you're trying to get a million things done before the semester starts. But try to answer their questions and give them the reassurance they need; give them as much time as you can. Some of these conversations can be delightful—after all, parents who sign their kids up for an improv class are usually pretty interesting people!

It will be easier to be friendly, helpful, and patient if you take a deep breath before you answer the phone and smile while you're talking. Even though they can't see the smile, they'll feel it through the phone and you'll feel more relaxed and generous.

If you have to call a parent to let them know something about their child during a time when that child is in class or camp, always start by letting them know that their child is okay. I usually start with, "Hi, this is Jessica from the Hideout—your child X is just fine. But I needed to call you today to let you know…." Even if their child is sick and needs to go home, or has gotten a bump or scrap, I still start off with saying that the child is fine, and then I let them know what the problem is. Phone calls from extra-curricular classes are very rare and you don't want to give the parents a heart attack while they wait for you to get to the real news of the situation!

Likewise, in this call you want to dispense with any pleasantries until after the problem has been dealt with. It may seem rude to skip the "How are you doing today?" But I assure you, the parents will appreciate it.

Face-to-Face Communication

You'll usually meet a parent or both parents on the first day of class (though the kids may be dropped off by another caregiver or if they're old enough, arrive on their own). When you meet them—even if it's the chaos of the first day of class—you want to take a moment to really look them in the eye and give them a firm handshake. Let them know you're happy that they and their child are there. Talk to the parent/s first, and then the child. This gives the parent the feeling that they're in charge of the situation and gives them a way to interact with you. But it also gives the child a chance to look you over, hear you speak, see how their parents interact with you, and generally get a feel for who you're before they have to interact with you. Kids can be quite nervous on the first day of class and you want to give them time to read the situation before you start asking them questions.

If you can manage it, it's best to have a person who is not a teacher check the kids in. In my early years, I would be doing everything. I would end up checking in a late child, or trying to take payment as the on-time kids were standing in a circle on stage getting really bored and restless. That's not a great way to start a class! Make sure to have all of your rosters printed out so that you can easily check people off and deal efficiently with all the parents. Also, make sure you know what the current payment situation is. It's much less awkward to ask about payment when they check in than at any other time.

I also like to come up with a little speech, something to tell them—maybe about parking or drop off, or it can even be something from the email I sent out—but I always say it to the parents as they're checking in on the first day. This little speech gives the parents a little more time to interact with you and get a feel for who you are. They usually feel reassured if you're telling them something they need to know, and they'll understand that you're professional and thoughtful, having foreseen some of their needs, and that you'll take care of them, and by extension, their children.

Parents will often ask if they can watch. I strongly recommend you do not allow this for any groups older than 8, and don't allow it past the first day for the younger kids. Children usually behave much better if they only have one authority figure to look to. If a parent is in the room, they may be checking in to make sure everything is okay with the parents first before they trust you. It makes the process of gaining their respect, and bonding the class as a whole, take much longer. Please learn from my experience of parents in class spilling coffee, calling their children over to discipline them, not leaving to take phone calls—parents in class just don't work.

For the little kids though, it's very hard for some of the parents to trust that their child's going to be okay. Letting them watch just the first 15 minutes of class can be a good way for them to see what the class will be like and to make sure their child is safe. Often the children will also feel reassured by their parents' presence, and this gives you time to gain their trust and show them how much fun class will be so they're okay when the parents go. And the parents rarely misbehave in that small amount of time!

With the parents of the older kids, I don't allow them in class at all. It's very disruptive and often embarrassing for their kids. The other kids will probably freeze up if they see that a strange adult is in the class. So it's best not to let them in. However, I do suggest that they can listen through the door if they like. They can often hear a lot of what is going on, but it's not super engaging so they don't usually stay beyond a few minutes. And I let them know there'll be a showcase at the end of the semester where they can see all the things their child has been doing.

Problems

No matter how well your program is set up and how good your teachers are, there will still be occasional problems.

When there is a problem with a child, or anything else related to the program, it's always best to deal with it as quickly as possible. You can choose email if there's not a lot of emotional content or you're dealing with financial matters. I like to inject humor whenever possible. Here is a recent email that I sent to a parent.

> Good Afternoon Parent,
>
> I notice that *Child* likes to wear Crocs—they look super comfortable. However, today in class, during a particularly spectacular piece of scene work, one of the Crocs came flying off and almost hit another child in the face. Fortunately, no one was hit, and everyone is fine.
>
> However, I feel that improv is risky enough without worrying about flying footwear. I'd really appreciate it if you would support *Child* to wear shoes that will stay attached to their feet.
>
> Thank you!

If the problem has more emotional content or if there's any chance the parent may challenge the program or the teacher, then it's best to call right away. Again, you want to start by letting them know their child is fine before you launch into the problem. Phone calls are best for situations like a child getting hurt during class, or if they're having a hard time and you need strategies, or if there is a problem with another child. All of these are difficult conversations, and it's best to have them on the phone or even in person if it's possible.

It's always best to be as kind and compassionate towards the parent as possible. No matter your struggles with a child, remember that a parent loves that child more deeply than anything in the world, and it's their job at times to be an unreasonable and unquestioning advocate for that child. So, deal gently but firmly with parents, by being very clear and setting appropriate boundaries. Usually the parents will work with you to improve the situation.

Some parents, like any people, will be difficult to deal with no matter what you do. With those people it's always best to be crystal clear, have strong boundaries and enforce everything, and ask for correctives as kindly and as neutrally as possible. I've even had parents who I assumed hated me and questioned everything about the program who later ended up being great advocates for my program, mainly because I figured out how to communicate clearly with them.

I have found that most parents are delightful, helpful, and excited to have their children learn from you. Taking an improv class is a pretty cool opportunity! With clear and frequent, timely communication, you will navigate most challenges easily and effectively.

CHAPTER ELEVEN

YOUR ALLIES? THE TEACHERS

If you have a good program and are professional, it won't take long until you'll need to start hiring teachers. Finding, training, and retaining good teachers can be a challenge, but once you create a good team, you'll be excited to see how other people teach and watch how their different styles create a more diverse program. I like the team aspect of teaching, and find other teachers to be a great resource for brainstorming about problems and new games. And it's just nice having other people around who are as passionate about teaching children as you are.

Finding Good Teachers

Your first step will be finding good teachers. This can be difficult because these teachers need to meet three criteria: first, to have enough improv experience to be able to teach the philosophies and games to someone else; second, experience teaching or managing children; and third and perhaps most especially, the right kind of energy. Imagine the Robin Williams character from *Dead Poets Society* or Ms. Frizzle from the *Magic School Bus* series, or Mary Poppins—someone who is playful and fun, but also able to say no and hold boundaries.

Just understanding the games and how to teach them will not be enough for a good program, even with a strong curriculum. You'll need someone who really understands and can explain the core principles of improv.

- They should feel deeply that fun is the core principle and everything else should stem from that.

- They really have to understand and accept "yes, and' to be able to teach it well. If they don't get it, then it becomes twisted into "never say no." Which is a very different thing, trust me.
- They need to get "be obvious" or else they will probably coach people into being clever, which leads to very shallow and short scenes.
- They should embrace the idea that the players are constantly and totally supporting one another on stage and that's how the process develops. Otherwise, they'll begin allowing some serious second-guessing and the kids will end up in the blame game.
- For any principle that you consider to be a core part of your program, the teachers should be not just on board, but enthusiastic proponents of that principle.

While you can discuss these principles and say you understand and get them, I find that it usually takes about 2-5 years of improv practice in your style of improv before people really get these concepts in a way that makes them able to coach them in other people. If you have a teacher with a strong understanding of these fundamentals, they'll be able to take your curriculum and make it work. They'll probably also be able to think outside the box and teach to the class that they have rather than just following the curriculum by rote. These are the teachers who can bring your program to life.

Next you'll need to consider the teacher's experience with kids. This is important. If they don't have some experience, then try making them a TA first before you promote them to teacher. Experience with kids is what enables the teachers to deal with the problems and different energies of various age groups. It's tempting to think that any nice person can handle kids, but I find that not to be true. When you hire people who are just nice, what you end up with is a roomful of howling monkeys and a burned-out teacher who refuses to come back. Not fun.

To really have a strong understanding of how kids at each age group work, you will want to have a teacher with at least a year of experience with the age group you're pairing them with, or a teacher with more experience with a different, but not dissimilar age group. For example, a preschool teacher can probably pretty easily take on a 5-8-year-old classroom, but might be baffled by middle school children. Though to be fair, middle school children are pretty baffling to most adults regardless of experience!

It's tempting to think that a teacher of adults can handle the teen classes, but even then, an experienced teen teacher will make a big difference in how well your teens learn and how much fun they have. Adult teachers tend to push the kids too fast and use setups that just don't work well for the teens. For example, "Okay, when the lights come up you're ex-husband and wife meeting after 10 years." Nope. Don't go there.

Finally, you'll need to consider the "energy" or personality of the teacher you're hiring. You'll need someone with:

- Energy to keep up with the kids
- Patience to help them learn
- Enthusiasm to keep them engaged
- The ability to be firm when necessary
- A measure of calm to be able to handle chaotic situations
- A goofy or silly side so they can play with the kids.

Once you have all of these elements in place, it'll be important to match the right teacher to the right age group. The best way to do this is to ask the teachers who they work well with—if they already have experience, they'll probably have a strong preference. Some teachers work really well with any age and that's great, but if they have an age limitation, respect that to make sure they stay effective and that their classes have the best possible time.

Setting Expectations

So you've found the perfect teacher! Congratulations! Now it's time to set expectations. Just as with the parents, clear, kind, frequent communication will go a long way in making sure that your teachers are happy and performing well.

Contracts

As soon as you agree to bring the teacher on board, get them a contract. I don't use this as a legal document, but rather as a tool to make sure everyone understands all the expectations. I will often email this to the teachers and ask them to read it and then just return the email with a line that they approve.

In the contract I lay out clearly:

- Who is hiring them—if it's me personally or the theater
- The dates and times of engagement
- The pay, how it's calculated, and when they will receive it
- What I expect from them in terms of teaching
- A statement that we can terminate them at any time for any reason
- And that we expect them to do whatever they can to make the program work well

Having them read and return this takes care of any questions that might come up later. It also sets the tone of you running a professional program.

Here is an example of my standard teacher contract:

The Hideout Theatre
Youth Program Teacher Contract

The Hideout Theatre is dedicated to developing a high-quality program of improv and performance instruction for youth. To facilitate this mission, the Hideout employs the most qualified teachers to meet or exceed our standards.

For this purpose, *Name* and the Hideout Theatre (the Hideout) agree to the following conditions of employment.

1) The dates of employment are *dates and days, weekly or daily, also times.*

2) You may ask for days off. Please be aware that you will be responsible for the class until a substitute can be found. Also, the first day of class, the week before the showcase, the showcase, and the last day of class are days that should not be missed unless you're ill.

3) The teacher agrees to serve the theater for the time of their contract, to perform duties as assigned, and to work cooperatively with the faculty and staff of the Hideout.

4) A general curriculum shall be provided to the teacher. Although the teacher may modify or add to the lessons, the general principles and core skills must be taught to each class.

5) The Hideout reserves the right to terminate this contract at any time. If terminated, the teacher will be compensated for all time and dates worked before the termination.

6) The Hideout agrees to pay a rate of *amount* per hour, to be paid on the 1st of the month immediately following the days worked. The teacher is responsible for turning in their hours by 5:00 pm of the 25th of each month to the General Manager.

7) Any changes to this document shall be made in writing and agreed to by both parties.

8) If the teacher has expenses, they must turn them into the General Manager and will be compensated in their paycheck (and are responsible for claiming the "reimbursements" as tax deductions).

Agreed:

________________________ _______________

Teacher Date

________________________ _______________

Director of Youth Programs Date

List of Expectations

In addition to this, it's good to have a list of expectations. These are things that you expect but they don't really go into the contract. Things you might want to address in this are:

- When teachers are expected to arrive
- Any perks they might have
- How to communicate while in class
- What to do if they need time off or get sick

- What your phone policy is
- If they need to clean up after class and how much

If you set these up in writing, then they're much more likely to be followed. Anything that's vital, or has been trouble in the past, you'll also want to address in person.

A good list of expectations can go a long way in making sure that you and your teachers have a strong working relationship.

Here is my list of expectations:

Appendix A: Teacher Duties

1) You're expected to follow the curriculum as long as it serves the class, and be willing and able to change directions if the class needs to review materials, try something different, or just needs a break.

2) You will help maintain the safe and pleasant atmosphere of the Hideout Theatre.

3) Please arrive no less than 10 minutes early for class and be ready to begin at the scheduled start time.

4) Please check your roster each day to ensure that all students are present. If someone is absent, email the parents to ask why. If they're gone more than two weeks in a row, let the Youth Director know.

5) If you anticipate needing a substitute, please give the Youth Director as much notice as possible. Be prepared to help find a sub by reaching out to other Hideout youth teachers to see if they can work for you.

6) You may need to write emails to the parents from time to time (to check in on an absent child, to help fill the classes by reaching out to your past students, etc.)

7) Inform the Youth Director of any problems that arise with any of the children, parents, theatre, other teachers, or anything that might affect the program.

8) Talk with parents as you come and go, but direct any serious questions to the Youth Director.

9) You will run the final showcase for your classes.

10) Your TA is in class to help you, but also to start learning how to be a teacher themselves. You should occasionally allow them to run a game or explain an important point if you feel they're capable.

11) Above all you should inspire your students with the joy and excitement of improv and help them to expand their own creativity and become the best performers and people they can be.

Meetings

A good amount of communication with your teachers will ensure that they feel supported and that they continue to run the classes in a way that works with your program. It also helps prevent burn-out, because you're giving them a place to vent frustrations as well as express their joys for the work.

You'll want to meet with your teachers to talk with them before you put them in a class. This is a place where you'll discuss their ideas and thoughts on the class as well as your expectations and wishes for the class. They will often have really good thoughts on the class and you don't want to miss out. This meeting should be casual and easy; I usually buy them coffee at a coffee shop.

If you go into this meeting with the idea that you're both on the same page and that you'll work together to make the best class possible, then you have set a great tone for your teacher's engagement with you.

In addition, you'll want to have occasional meetings with them throughout the year. A casual and short meeting about a month after they've started gives them a chance to bring up any difficulties they're having and to clarify anything they might be confused with. It also gives them a chance to talk about their kids. Generally, teachers really love their kids and will tell you about funny things they did. If they're doing this spontaneously, then you know you have someone who is a good fit in terms of enjoying the work and being excited to play with the kids. This doesn't have to be an official meeting—if they have time after class you can just catch up with them then. That makes it feel less like supervision and more like you're just there for them.

Training

Training new teachers is really fun and exciting. It's great to share your passion for teaching with someone who is just discovering it. Make sure they have all the tools they need to do a great job when they're in charge of a class by themselves.

The best way is to have them co-teach a class with you or with another trusted teacher. Start off teaching the class on your own, with them observing. After each class, check in with them to see if they have questions or thoughts on the class.

Then start having them lead games. At this point you'll be tempted to correct and jump in. As much as possible, sit back and let them develop their style. Unless they're telling the kids something totally wrong, you don't need to correct them there. Just trust that you will cover all the material in several ways, so if the kids don't get it this way, they will get it soon. You can talk about how the games went during your check-in. At that point you can offer advice and ways to handle things differently, as well as let them know what they did well and should continue to keep doing.

After they're solid in running games, you can have them start explaining concepts, and then teaching the games that illustrate those concepts. As you let them lead the games, try to sit back and allow them to work their way through the material. You can add small comments as long as they're brief and don't undercut the new teacher. And then, work out the details during the check-in later.

Finally, let them take an entire class, teach it by themselves, and just be there to offer backup and assistance. You'll want to give them a solid curriculum for the day so they know what they're doing. But remind them that ultimately they will need to respond to the needs of the class in the moment. If the curriculum says to do a quiet concentration game, but the kids are too squirrely for that at the moment, they'll have to see if there is a better game to substitute or if they can come up with their own thing to put in place for that moment.

Ultimately, the teacher is there to make the class run, and their job is to figure out how best to keep everyone happy and learning. The curriculum's there as a support and guideline and best used that way, with lots of latitude for creating a class that makes sense in the moment.

Once you feel they've gotten good enough at running classrooms, you can let them have a class on their own. If you can give them a good solid TA, it helps. But either way, frequent check-ins will be very helpful in making sure they're supported and feel confident in their role.

Overall, setting very strong and clear expectations in every aspect of their role will help you support and maintain happy, high-quality teachers. And as teachers are a fundamental part of your program, you'll want to do everything you can to have the best-trained teachers possible.

Good Communication

Good and frequent communication is a must for maintaining a healthy program. Teachers need to be supported and to vent from time to time. Good communication allows them to talk to someone who understands and helps to head off problems before they become too difficult. It also allows teachers to revel in their enjoyment regarding their classes. There are few people who understand how fun and exciting it is to teach improv to children, so they don't have that many people with whom to share their joy. If you ask about the awesome aspects of classes from time to time, they get a chance to relive their favorite moments and strengthen their love for teaching.

Email — I find that email is great for things that need to be addressed quickly, but don't have much of an emotional component. A new kid is joining class, reminders about skipping a holiday, or checking in to see if they want to teach for the next semester—these are all things that are perfect for email.

Face-to-Face — For problems that have an emotional component or that may be complex, a phone call or face-to-face check-in is better. If a child is difficult, or a parent was contentious, or they have a problem with another teacher, they will probably want to vent a little, and get support and reassurance. Once they feel more confident, it's easier to resolve issues.

For very difficult or emotional subjects, always aim for a face-to-face. You'll want to ask them open-ended questions about the subject and then really listen to what they're saying, resisting the urge to interrupt, unless you need clarification, and then only briefly. Once you feel like they've gotten all their feelings out, you can reassure them and support them. Once they know you're not going to yell at them or fire them (assuming you're not going to yell at them or fire them!), then they can relax enough to work on the problem. If you try problem-solving first then you'll have to deal with their anxieties and defensiveness throughout the discussion. Better to deal with the emotions first, then problem-solving will be much easier and very likely the solution will become clear.

Check-ins — Communication should not happen just when there are problems or when you need to share information. If you can make sure there are occasional casual encounters, this is the best. You'll be able to support, validate, problem-solve, and correct in a casual and low-stress situation.

Formal Meetings — However, every teacher, even the established ones, should have at least one formal meeting during the year. This is a time to let them know how they're doing. Make sure to accentuate the positive more than the negative. You want them to know that you value them and support them as a teacher. This will make it easier for them to bring you concerns and let you know how they're doing.

Good communication will create an environment where your teachers feel validated, supported, and cared for. In an environment like this, they will be able to perform better and be the best teachers they can be.

Problems

No teacher is going to be completely unproblematic. After all, they're humans and humans are complex creatures with many conflicting needs and desires. When dealing with any teacher problems, it's best to assume that they want to be doing their best and want to be a great teacher for the kids. If you come from that perspective, then you'll be on the same team looking for solutions together, rather than an authority figure telling them what they need to do and/or expecting them to figure it out on their own.

Tardy — Being tardy is a common problem. Improvisors tend to run on "Improv Time." I ask teachers to show up 10 minutes early so that they're ready for class. This works for a large portion of people and will at least get them there before the class starts. If they still have a hard time showing up on time for class, then I ask them what's making it hard. Usually if we can discuss it a little we'll come up with solutions, but even more importantly it reinforces for them how important it is to show up on time. It's slightly embarrassing, but if you do it in a supportive way, they typically respond well.

If it's still a problem, then explain to them that this is an absolute. They just can't show up after the start time—no matter how good they're as a teacher, I'll need to find someone else. I rarely fire people, but I will not rehire someone who cannot be on time.

Taking Too Much Time Off— Everyone gets sick from time to time. And everyone will need a week off now and then. If a teacher is only teaching on Saturdays, then I assume they'll get sick about once or twice a year, and further will need to miss one or two classes for personal reasons. Missing more than three or four classes in a year is a problem. Remember that in my program, they only teach for 28 days total, so missing four is a lot.

First off, you'll want to make sure they're not burning out and losing their enthusiasm for the job. If they're, then you'll need to address that first. Either help them find a way to become excited about the work again, or help them figure out that they need a break from teaching for now. It's a hard thing to decide, because people do love it so much and miss being with the kids, but if it's time to move on, the best thing to do is move on. Usually, if they know they'll finish out the semester and be done, that's enough to get them through. Having the end in sight can be really helpful.

If they're burning out, then they may be getting sick from the kids. I like to encourage people to wash their hands after working with kids and take extra hygiene precautions. Kids are full of nasty germs, and if you're not used to them, you can pick up a lot of illnesses. Usually, this is a one semester problem, and the teachers get stronger immune systems pretty quickly.

Parent Complaints — There will be parent complaints from time to time. I was very lucky that my first complaint I received was about me—the parent did not know that the "sub" was actually the director. I learned a lot from that complaint. First off, I learned that you should listen to parents and thank them for their input. Parents may complain for a number of reasons, only some of which may actually be the teacher's fault. However, no matter what they're complaining about, it's important to listen and take their concerns seriously. Even if you can do nothing about their struggle, they will feel much better if they feel heard and believed.

In the complaint about me, it was a case of me not communicating with their regular teacher about what she had been doing and how she was running the classroom. I assumed that since I was a great teacher and had run many classes, I could simply swoop in and take over. However, she had set her little guys up in a way that they expected certain things and they were confused and discombobulated when they didn't happen. This was a very young class of 5-8-year-olds and the teacher had allowed the parents to sit in, which made it even harder to control the class—when they didn't have their normal teacher, they looked to the parents for guidance instead of me. The entire hour was a struggle, with me trying to maintain control and desperately figuring out how to make this class fun for these little guys without any of them breaking an arm.

As much as I didn't like the complaint, I did learn some really important things: first, always get a full picture of the class, what they're working on and their favorite games, from the main teacher; second, never let parents watch; and third, I'm not the best teacher for 5-8-year-olds.

Once you have heard and understood the parent/s, it's time to assess the complaint. Is this a serious complaint that needs immediate attention? Is there something in this that the teacher could address? Or is there another way to handle this, for instance in changing something about the structure of the program? Or is it a miscommunication in the program?

Then you can talk to the teacher. I always talk to the teacher even if it's nothing they can change, because I think it's important for them to know what's happening in the student/s environment. If it really is nothing, let them know that right up front, then share what the complaint was and let them talk about it a bit. They will probably need to defend themselves. Make sure you let them know that you have their back and they're not in trouble.

If it's something more serious, bring up the subject and then wait and let them talk. Make sure you really understand what they're saying and what their perspective is. Once they've fully shared, you can offer feedback and guidance for how to deal with the situation. Assure them again that their job is not threatened, and that you'll work with them to create the best possible outcome.

Not Following the Curriculum — Every lesson should have room for improvisation. You want your teachers to be able to use their talents, experience, and intelligence to make a great class. However, there will be times when you get push-back on specific portions of the curriculum. There will be times when the ideas are good, and you'll either want to give that teacher full reign to explore them, or perhaps incorporate them into everyone's curriculum.

However, for the health of your program, it's necessary for the teachers to teach some basic essential concepts. The best way to make sure this happens is to mark it in the curriculum. I highlight anything that's not optional. That applies to both games that you want to make sure the kids know and concepts that are important to convey. If the concept is highlighted, then the teacher knows that needs to be taught and they can structure the rest of the class around that.

Sometimes you'll get a teacher who just doesn't know all the concepts you're teaching, usually because they come from a different improv tradition. In that case, I have them shadow me while I teach the concepts to a class. Or—and this is a fun option—because there's an adult program at my theatre, I offer to let them take the full range of classes so they can learn our improv style.

If the teacher understands the concept at hand, but just doesn't want to teach it for philosophical reasons, then that's an indication that this teacher isn't a good fit. It might be better to let them teach a class in specific topics, or an advanced class, rather than allow them to teach at the basic level and have your kids being taught radically different approaches.

Lack of Enthusiasm — It's late in the semester, the teacher is complaining more often and has a hard time showing up or showing up on time. When they teach, they teach like a robot, following the lessons, but not adding any enthusiasm. You may be dealing with burnout. I know this personally. There have been times when I'm just not excited about teaching. The first thing to figure out is if there's something specific making it difficult for them—for example, is their class too early in the morning? I actually moved the start time for my entire program back to 10:00 am because I had a hard time finding improvisors who could be awake and excited at 9:00 am on a Saturday.

Once you know their struggle, it's easy to work with it. It's harder if they're just tired of teaching. Usually at that point, what they really need is time off. If you can find a sub for a week or two, that might do wonders. You might also just need to let them take a semester off. It's amazing how much more fun it's to teach children when you're fresh and rested.

Don't let a lack of enthusiasm continue for longer than a few weeks—it's pretty deadly to a classroom. The kids pick up on it and will start being uninterested as well. It's best to take care of this as soon as possible.

When dealing with any of these problems, you might need to talk to the TA to get their perspective. They will feel bad if they're "telling on" their teacher/co-worker, so tread lightly and gently. Let them know there's a problem and that you need their perspective. And then just listen and get a full understanding of what they see and hear in class.

If you do have to let a teacher go, do it as quickly and with as little emotion as possible. It does no one any good to drag it out and keep people in uncertainty. Let them know the reason, and then let them know they're terminated and when and how they'll get their last paycheck. Usually, if a teacher isn't working out, they will know it. It's a hard decision, but if it needs to happen, better to handle it and move on.

Ultimately, if you have clear communication and treat your teachers like you're all team members working towards the same awesome goal, then you will have an effective and enthusiastic staff.

CONCLUSION

GO GET 'EM TIGER!

I have now taught hundreds, maybe even thousands of kids. Kids who are neurotypical, kids who are on the autism spectrum, kids who are succeeding, kids who are struggling, kids who have difficult home lives and kids who are already so happy that their joy overflows in every class. Every once in a while, you'll find a child, or more likely teen, who is just not interested in playing and that's okay. But that's the exception—the vast, vast majority of kids love improv.

Most of them start off by loving the games—the games are so much fun! Then they'll find other aspects of improv that excite them. Some of the kids are captivated by characters and love creating silly or grounded or outrageous characters to people the stage. Others delve into storytelling and get very excited about the different beats of a story and how to make conflict happen and what a cohesive narrative arc looks like. You'll find some for whom timing becomes an obsession and others who delight in pun games. There are so many delightful aspects to improv that it can take years to fully explore all that the art has to offer.

Every so often, I'll get a note from one of my former students. They tell me how important improv is to them, how it has helped them achieve success, or let me know how well they're doing and how fondly they remember their time in improv.

They are thanking me, but really the thanks go to the art of improv. This is a powerful tool that, in the right hands, can help create stronger, more authentic, more joyful adults.

Thank you for reading this book and for your interest in teaching improv to children and teens. Your job will be to help guide the next generation into a world that is ever changing and often unpredictable.

Having the tools of improv will allow them to negotiate those changes with grace and joy. This is the job of each generation—like Girl Scouts, we are charged with leaving the world a little better than we found it.

As you go, a final word of advice: This book is meant only as a guide, a reference book, and a tool. You are the teacher or the program director, and it's up to you to assess the needs of your kids, parents, teachers, and program. This book will be useful in giving you guidance. But in the end, teaching is about relationships and about giving of yourself to someone else. I can't do that for you. I can only provide a flashlight to illuminate the journey and make it a little easier for you.

As I write this conclusion, it is the end of 2020, and the world looks very different from when I started my improv journey, or even when I started this book! Thanks to my improv training, I have been able to adjust, both personally and professionally, to the changing demands of our current world.

Ultimately these are some of the benefits of improv—the ability to be flexible, to meet changing situations, and to take the risks necessary to find success and delight in a world that might be very different from one day to the next.

I wish each of you joy and growth as you navigate your improv teaching journey! Go get 'em, tiger!

INDEX OF GAMES

Adjective Circle

Warm-up
Name game

Have the children stand in a circle. Go around the circle and have each child make up an adjective to go with their name—such as "Serious Sarah." When they say their name, the entire circle says it back to them. After everyone has an adjective, break them into pairs and have them give each other a gesture that goes with their adjective. Go around the big circle again, where each child will say their adjective name and gesture, and all the others will repeat it.

Once they have that down, have them say their name and do their gesture and then say the name and do the gesture of another child in the circle. That child will say their name and do their gesture and continue to pass it on.

Alien Translator

Performance Game

One person is the alien, one person the translator, and one person the host. The Alien speaks only in gibberish, the translator "translates" (makes up) what the Alien has said, and the host asks questions. It's important to make sure that the "alien" doesn't "correct" the translator. The whole point is sharing control. Make sure that the "host" gets questions from the audience as well. Then it's fun to change things up and have the three take new roles.

This game is great for an introduction to how improv works.

Alphabet

Performance Game

Have two kids on stage. They're just having a normal scene, but each line must begin with the next letter of the alphabet.

For example:
"Alright, we're ready to fly!"
"Bandana's ON!"
"Can you give me the yellow bandana?"
"Do you want me to put it on you?"
Etc.

For kids 10 and under, start with A. For older kids start in the middle of the alphabet. This is a great game for getting kids to be more relaxed about their scene work.

Ball

Warm-up
Bonding

Have a very soft ball. It can be plastic or cloth—in fact, I often use a balloon for this. Have the kids stand in a circle and throw the ball out. At first the only rule is to keep it off the ground. Then you can add rules, like:

You can't hold the ball
You can only touch it once before someone else must touch it
You have to make silly noises when you touch the ball
You count together each time someone touches it

If the ball touches the ground, everyone says "Awwwww..." and you pick it up and start again. Don't let them blame each other or themselves—just pick it up and start again.

Blind Line

Performance Game

Set up: Have the audience write words or short phrases on slips of paper. These are scattered on the floor of the stage. Then have two to three children come up and perform a scene. At random points during the scene, the children should pick up a piece of paper and use that word or phrase in the scene. At first you can have the kids look at the word and figure out how to use it. When you want to make it more challenging, have them say the word as soon as they see it and then justify why they said that. As the scene goes on, they should go to the paper more and more frequently.

This is a great game for helping kids be spontaneous.

Blind Trust Walks

Exercise
Bonding

Only do this if you trust the children to take care of each other. Have the children in pairs. One child closes their eyes and keeps them closed. The other child stands behind them with their hands on the blind child's shoulders. They will gently guide the blind child with taps to let them know where they need to go. The child in front controls the speed of the movement. The child behind is only helping them get places and making sure they don't get into trouble. The guiding child is allowed to say things like "step up" or "slow down" or whatever else they need to say to make sure the blind child is safe. After about 5 minutes, have the children switch roles.

This game is great for building trust and learning how to take care of your partner.

Bunny and Fox

Warm-up
Bonding

It's the same game as **Cat and Mouse**. Have the children in pairs holding both hands in such a way as to form a "bunny hole" between them. One child is a bunny and one child is a fox. The fox chases the bunny. If the fox catches the bunny then the bunny becomes the fox and starts chasing the child who was the fox and who has now become the bunny. At any point the bunny can duck into a "bunny hole" and take the hands of one of those children. At that point the bunny has now become part of the bunny hole. The child who was displaced becomes the bunny and runs from the fox. You'll need to really push the bunnies to take the hands of only one child so that it's really clear who is the new bunny and who remains the bunny hole. If you have a very fast child, you'll need to coach them to choose a bunny hole rather than just run around evading the fox. Coach them to go fast and switch often so that they all get a chance to play. This game is great for overcoming cliques as it forces the kids to have different partners.

Bunny Bunny

Warm-up

Have the children in a circle. Stress that the rhythm of this game is important. Have all the children start by saying "Who, Ha, Who, Ha." On each syllable they will touch one knee then the other. This will continue the entire game. Then one child will say "Bunny, Bunny," while making bunny ears with their fingers at themselves and then "Bunny, Bunny," while making bunny ears at another child. The child who was pointed at will then take up the chant saying "Bunny, Bunny," while making bunny ears at themselves. Once they have that going well, add the next layer. When a child is saying "Bunny, Bunny, Bunny, Bunny," the children on each side of that child will be saying "Tokee, Tokee, Tokee, Tokee," while holding their arms out and waving them up and down. You will have three things going on—"Who, Ha, Who, Ha," "Bunny, Bunny, Bunny, Bunny," and "Tokee, Tokee, Tokee, Tokee." These should all be in rhythm so that each syllable is said at the same time. It usually starts out slow and then ends up going very fast.

This game is great for building energy and connection.

Bus Stop

Performance Game

Have a bench set up on the stage. One child takes the stage and waits at the bus stop, and another child joins. They will have a scene, and the first child to laugh or "break" has to leave the scene and then a new child joins. You'll have to coach them to try to be big and silly. Be careful because sometimes this game can also just reward behavior that you don't necessarily want, like being scary or surprising instead of engaging in the scene.

This is great for the kids who really want to show off because it gives them a chance to do that in an appropriate manner, but also rewards being aware of your partner.

Cat and Mouse

Warm-up
Bonding

This is the same game as **Bunny and Fox** just with different names. Have the children in pairs holding both hands in such a way as to form a "mouse hole" between them. One child is a mouse and one child is a cat. The cat chases the mouse. If the cat catches the mouse then the mouse becomes the cat who starts chasing the child who was the cat and has now become the mouse. At any point the mouse can duck into a mouse hole and take the hands of one of those children. At that point the mouse has now become part of the mouse hole. The child who was displaced becomes the mouse and runs from the cat. Push the mice to take the hands of only one child so that it's really clear who is the new mouse and who remains the mouse hole. If you have a very fast child, you'll need to coach them to choose a mouse hole rather than just run around evading the cat. Coach them to go fast and switch often so that they all get a chance to play.

This game is great for overcoming cliques as it forces the kids to have different partners.

Category Die

Performance Game

Have the children in a row, shoulder to shoulder, facing the front of the stage. You designate a category such as "Pizza Toppings." You point to the children in random order, and as you point at them they must list a pizza topping. If they hesitate, repeat a previous offer, or say something wrong you say "Die" and they pretend to die dramatically and must go sit down. For the younger children, instead of "Die," the audience claps twice and says "Outta There!"

The game is meant to teach saying things quickly and off the cuff. You should go quickly so that they don't have time to preload more than the first one. If you give them time to think that defeats the purpose of the game.

Also point out that you can be wrong and call people out unjustly, and you can miss people who should have been called out. The other kids will be tempted to point out when someone makes a mistake, but don't let them—keep the game going and let them know that for this game it's all of them against the director.

This game is great for settling kids down after getting too energetic. For kids who need to be "right" this game gives them both the satisfaction of being right and practice with things going awry.

Character Advice

Performance Game

This is very similar to **Good, Bad, Worse Advice**. Have four children sit on stage. This is set up like an advice show, with one host and three guests. The host will ask questions—either their own or questions from the audience. The host should start with introductions so each guest is able to show off the character they have chosen. Each of the three guests have very different characters or personalities. Each guest will answer the same question, but will offer their own perspective.

Tell the kids that this is a great game for working on contrast—listening to your fellow improvisors so that you can offer something different. For very young children, I have them pick different animals and they answer from the animals' perspective. This is a great way to have them start building characters that are different from themselves.

This is a great game for developing characters and working on contrast.

Character Explosion

Exercise

Have the kids standing on the back line or on the sides of the stage. One kid (Kid A) will stay on stage, in the same basic character for the whole game. The game starts with Kid A and one other kid on stage doing a short scene, maybe 30 seconds. Someone yells "Freeze" and comes in. The partner in the scene leaves, and this new kid will now start a new scene with Kid A, but they'll be playing someone else from that character's life. That scene is brief and then someone else yells "Freeze" and comes in as yet a different person from the character's life. For example:

Kid A is Lisa, a middle school child.

The first scene partner is Lisa's Mom.

The second scene partner is Mrs. Gomez, Lisa's teacher.

The third scene partner is Jane, Lisa's best friend.

This continues until you feel satisfied. You can either end the game or bring in another kid to maintain a new character on the stage and have the kids play new roles in this character's life.

This game is good for exploring character and for developing scene work.

Character Switch

Performance Game

Two children will be on stage performing a scene. When you ring a bell or say "Switch" then the children will switch places and take on the character of the other child. Continue switching them back and forth faster and faster until it has a silly ending.

This is a great game for kids who are too clever or are unable to work well with partners.

Color/Advance

Exercise

Have the children in pairs. One child will be telling a story. At any point the other child can say "Color" and the first child will have to provide details about the story. They should continue telling the details and describing the scene until the other child says "Advance." At that point the storyteller will go back to describing the plot. They will continue until the other child says "Color" again or until the story is over.

You also have the option of adding in "Emotion." At that point the storyteller will tell how people were feeling during this portion of the story.

When the story ends, the children should switch and allow the other child to be the storyteller.

This is great for showing kids how much the audience wants more than just the next thing.

Come Over Here If

Warm-up
Bonding

The children are milling around an open space. One child says "Come over here if ..." and they say something that's true for them, such as "You like cats." Then the rest of the children stand near the child according to how true that is for them. So if it's very true for them then they stand right next to the child. If they don't like cats at all then they stand far away. It's up to each child to decide where they stand and what that means for them.

This is great for kids who are having a rough time with each other.

Commercials

Performance Game

At the front of the stage have two chairs or boxes set up to create the "tv screen." The children stand in a line to the back or side of the stage. You sit in the audience pretending to surf channels. As you say "Click" or "Next," the next child comes up and does their part of a commercial or tv show or newscast. You should keep this going very fast, like only 3-5 seconds each, unless they have something really good and want to keep going. When they're done, they either sit down or go back in line for another round.

This is great for kids who need more time to come up with ideas. It also reinforces that nothing is very precious.

Convergence

Warm-Up
Bonding

Have the kids in a circle. Each kid will try to think of a random word. Once they have a word, they say "One." When another kid thinks of their own word they will say "Two." Then these two kids together will say "One, Two, Three…" and then each say their own word simultaneously. After that each kid will try to think of another word that is between the two words that were just said. When one of them thinks of a word they will say "One." Again, when a second kid thinks of a word, that kid will say "Two." Then together both kids will say "One, Two, Three…" and they each say their own word simultaneously. Usually the words are still different and the game continues. If they manage to say the same word, they have reached convergence and you celebrate by pretending to be robots and chanting "Convergence" three times. For example:

Child A: One
Child B: Two
Together: One, Two Three
Child A: Tree Child B: Fly
Child C: One
Child D: Two
Together: One Two Three
Child C: Bird Child D: Bird
Everybody: Convergence, Convergence, Convergence

This is a great game for concentration and for getting the kids to work together.

Creating Machines

Performance Game
Bonding

Have the children stand off the stage. One child enters and starts making a gesture and a noise. These should be things they can repeat for a long while. A second child joins them and adds onto the first child, making their own gesture and noise. One at a time you have all the children join until you have a full machine. At that point it's fun to have them slow down or speed up or turn gravity off, or make it a scared machine. It's always fun to end with the machine breaking apart one child at a time.

This is great for kids who are having a hard time working together.

Creating Shapes With Paper

Exercise

Have a bunch of strips of paper, approximately 2 inches by 4 inches. Have the children sitting in a close circle of three to five children. Give the strips to the children and show them that they can lay them down to create shapes. The children should take turns around the circle to create an interesting shape or pattern. No one may move or take out something that's already laid down. Once they're done, take a picture of these creations so the children feel some finality. Then have them push the papers altogether. There is something satisfying about destroying your creation and this helps them to see how it feels to create something and then let it go.

This is a great exercise for kids who are tired and need a rest.

Dance Diamond

Performance Game

Have some fun, upbeat music playing. Have the children on the stage, one in front, one to the right about midway back, one to the left about midway back, and one at the very back. As the music plays, the child in front will dance and the other children will follow their motions, copying them as closely as possible. When the front child is tired of being in charge, they will turn towards one of the other children, thus making all the children turn so that they're all facing the same way and putting a new child "in front." That child will dance, and the others will follow them until they turn as well. Continue until it feels like everyone has had enough time as the leader. You'll need to coach them to go slowly so that the other kids can follow them.

This is a great game for wrapping things up and audiences love it.

Dwarf Wizard Giant

Warm-up

Have the kids in two teams on opposite sides of the room. In secret they will need to decide if they want to be Dwarfs (in which case they will get low and hold their hands on their beards), Wizards (in which case they will hold their hands out in front as if they're casting a spell), or Giants (in which case they will get as tall as they can and hold their hands up in the air as if they're really tall). Once they've made the decision, then they let you know they're ready to go—this decision should be secret from the other group of kids.

As a group you will all chant "Ki-nick, Ki-nak, Ki-nick, Ki-nak, Ki-nick, Ki-nak GO." As they're chanting this, they walk like their normal kid selves to the middle of the stage, and when you say "GO," they show which type of character they are—Dwarf, Wizard, or Giant.

Giants will win over Wizards, Wizards will win over Dwarfs, and Dwarfs will win over Giants—because they trip them.

The group of children who "won" will keep their feet planted, but will try to use their arms to tag the kids in the losing group. Every child they tag will now become part of the winning group. If both sides do the same gesture then they just shake hands and say "Good morning to you!" Keep playing as long as it's fun.

This is a great game for regaining control if there has been some chaos. It also forces the kids to work together nicely.

Elevator

Performance Game

Have one child on stage. This child pretends to get onto an elevator—if possible, they should still have a pretty strong character even though they're by themselves. After a few seconds a second child comes to the elevator with a different character. The first child takes on this new character—they might retain their own concerns and ideas, but they'll copy the way the other child talks and stands. Then a third child comes into the elevator and the other two take on this child's character. Finally, a fourth arrives and they all take on that character. Then the fourth child gets off the elevator and all the children go back to the third child's character. Then this child gets off and they all go back to the second child's character. Continue this until you're left with only the original child.

This is a great game for working on character. It also forces kids to do something different from their go-to characters.

Enemy Defender

Warm-up
Bonding

Everyone secretly picks two people (one enemy and one defender). When the game starts, your goal is to move around so that your defender is always between you and your enemy. Let the game go for as long as people are laughing and engaged. You can then switch it up and have the kids try to make an equilateral triangle with two new people. You can also have the kids try to put themselves between their enemy and defender—this is actually impossible for everyone to achieve, but it leads to some fun jostling.

This game is great for bringing up the energy.

Evolution

Warm-up

Have the kids in a circle. The first child turns towards one of the children next to them and makes a sound and gesture. The child next to them takes that in and turns to the next child and tries to copy what they saw. This child will then copy what they saw and it continues. You'll need to make sure they're copying what they saw in the child who gave it to them and not trying to go back to the original sound and gesture. They have a tendency to think that the original is "right" and that they need to get back to that. Instead you're aiming to have the sound and gesture morph and change naturally, without adding things in, just letting it change and then noting how much it changes just around the circle.

Some fun variations are to ask the first child to start as small as possible and then have each subsequent child do it just a little bit bigger. And, of course, the opposite—have the children start big and see how small they can make it.

This is a classic and frequently used improv warm-up because it emphasizes listening, speaking with your own voice, and letting things evolve naturally.

Eyes on Paper

Exercise
Bonding

Have the children in pairs. Give them each a different colored marker. Then give the pair one piece of paper that has two dots for eyes drawn on it. The children must together create a portrait by each taking turns making a line on the paper. They're allowed to make something big, like the ear, but they can't use the line to create more than one segment of the face.

This is great for tired children.

Five Things

Exercise

Have the kids in a circle. One child says to the child next to them, "Give me five __________ (things in a category)." The child responds by listing any five things that come into their brain—the point is to go quickly, not to be correct. As they list them the rest of the group counts after each one.

"Give me five pizza toppings."
"Pepperoni."
"One."
"Cheese."
"Two."
"Popcorn."
"Three."
"Crust."
"Four."
"Motor Oil."
"Five—Five things!"

This game is great for kids who have to be right as it lets them play with being more spontaneous.

Foreign Film

Performance Game

Have two children at the front of the stage. They will be the translators. Have two children in the stage area. They're the actors. When the scene starts, the actors will speak only gibberish while acting out the scene. After each line, the translators will translate. Have a translator assigned to each actor so they know who is translating for whom. You'll need to coach them to make the translation match the actors' tone and gestures.

This game is great for being obvious and being aware of what your scene partner is doing.

Freeze

Performance Game

Have the children along the back wall of the stage area. Two children come out and start a scene, and at some point, you or another child will yell "Freeze!" Both of the children who are performing freeze in their positions. Then the child who yelled "Freeze" comes out and taps one of the children in the scene on the shoulder—that child will go back to the line and the tapping child will take their place and will copy the physical stance of the child who just left. Then this new child will start a new scene from that stance. They cannot reference something that was said in the last scene, but must start a completely new scene from the same position.

This is great for building montage skills.

Freeze Dance

Exercise

Put on some fun music to dance to. If you have them, let the kids hold scarves. They will dance until you stop the music, then they freeze in place. If anyone moves while the music is stopped then they're out. If anyone doesn't dance, they're also out. Encourage them to take risks with this.

This is great for kids who need to get some energy out.

Fortunately/Unfortunately

Performance Game

Start with one child standing at the front right of the stage—this is the Angel. Another child will stand at the front left of the stage—this is the Devil. The other two children will be the actors in the scene. Start the scene by getting some kind of adventure for the actors. The two kids in the middle will start the scene, but nothing much should happen—they should mostly establish location and relationship. Then the Angel will say "Fortunately," and will give them something good or fun in the scene. The two actors will react to this physically and verbally for a bit. Then the Devil will say "Unfortunately," and will give them something bad in the scene. The actors will react to this as well.

This is a great game for sharing control and separating out plot from details and reactions. You will need to coach the actors not to push the plot forward, but just to wait for something to happen to them. Also, you'll need to coach the Angel and Devil not to just undo what the last person said, but to work on something different. As in most scenes, it's really fun to start slow and then have the Angel and Devil speed up at the end.

This is a great game for kids who are not yet able to develop a scene on their own.

Genre/Emotional Zones

Performance Game

Before the game starts ask the audience for three different genres or emotions. Then designate ⅓ of the stage for each emotion or genre. For maximum fun, make them as different from each other as possible. Have the children start in different "zones." As they play the game, they should frequently move from one zone to the next and try to justify their new reactions.

This is a great game for kids who only play one character or emotion.

Good Bad Worst Advice

Performance Game

Have four children sit on stage. This is like an advice show where you have one host and three guests. The host should start with introductions so each guest is able to show off the character they have chosen. The host will ask questions—either their own or questions from the audience. The guests will play three different roles. The first guest will give good advice. This is a great position for the hesitant kid, the shy kid, or the kid who has a hard time being wrong. The second kid will give bad advice. This is just advice that goes against common sense or feels really wrong. This position is great for the mischievous kid. The last position will give terrible advice. This position is perfect for kids who like big silly characters and for those that have extra energy. This is a heightening game, so you want good advice to be actually pretty good; bad advice is bad, but still within rational bounds; and worst advice should really be out of context or just plain bizarre.

This is a great game for showing off fun characters and for learning about heightening.

Hell Dub

Performance Game

Start with three children on stage. The first child provides the voice for the second, but maintains their own body character. The second child provides the voice for the third, and the third provides the voice for the first. As the scene goes on, the children should continue providing the voice for the same person, but then try to move their mouth and body as if they were speaking when someone is speaking for them. This is super difficult and super fun both, and requires the kids to share control.

This is a great game for when the kids need a challenge.

Helping Hands

Performance Game

Start with two children on stage. They have their hands on their hips. Two other children will each pick one child to be the arms for. They will stand behind the one of the children who has their hands on their hips and thread their arms through the hole left between the other child's side and arms on the hips. Then the child in back will be the arms for the child in front. The child in front will be responsible for talking and basically carrying the scene forward, but the child in back will be the one to make any hand gestures. Try to make the suggestions for this scene something where you would naturally use your hands a lot.

This game is great for children who need to explore improvising without talking.

Hesitation Debate

Performance Game

Start with two children standing on stage. They will get a suggestion of a small and unimportant thing to debate. One child will start by arguing for the topic. From time to time that child will hold out their hand and the audience will give them a word. The child then must immediately use that word in their speech. When it's the other child's turn, they will provide the against argument. As they go back and forth, they should go to the audience more and more often, making it increasingly ridiculous. For example:

Child: "I think playgrounds are great because" [sticks out hand]
Audience: "Cheese Sticks!"
Child: "Cheese sticks are an important part of childhood and playgrounds are where you find cheese sticks."

They should do their best to justify the suggestion even if it's totally ridiculous. Go for three rounds of back and forth. Try to make the kids go to the audience at least three of four times per round.

This is a great game for the kids who are very clever and need some challenge. It is also a game that keeps everybody engaged.

House-Creature-Flood

Warm-up

Have the kids in groups of three. Two kids will hold each other's hands above their heads making a house. The third child will be between the two kids in the "house." This child in the middle should try to look like a ridiculous creature. One child will be the caller. If the caller says "House," then the children making houses will disengage and go find other children to be houses with other creatures. Very important, the "creatures" should not move and the "houses" should form over a creature, not off by themselves. If the caller calls out "Creature," then the "creatures" move and try to change houses. Again, the houses should not move. If the caller calls "Flood," then all the children should disengage and reform as either a house or a creature. Don't move on until everyone is in a new formation. In all cases, the caller should try to join in either as a house or a creature and then whomever is left out should become the new caller.

This is a great game to play when the children need to get out some energy.

Hype Man

Performance Game

Two children are playing a normal scene, but a third child stands behind one of the players and only affirms and accentuates what that child is saying.

Child 1: "Let's go to the store."
Hype Man: "That's right—the STORE! It's the place to be!"
Child 2: "Okay that sounds like fun."
Child 1: "We can get bananas."
Hype Man: "Oh man, bananas! We're going to get some potassium!"

For children who are very shy or hesitant, put them in the Child 1 spot. It is super fun for them to have everything they say be validated right away.

I Am a Tree

Exercise

The children stand in a circle or on the back line of the stage. The first child comes out and says "I am a tree" and takes the shape of a tree, then the next child comes out and adds something to the picture/scene—for example, "I am an apple," while pretending to hold an apple under the tree. Then a third child comes out and completes the picture/scene. For example, they might say "I am a worm in the apple." Then the first child decides which of the other two will stay by saying "I will leave the worm." The other two children leave the circle and the child who said they were a worm stays. That child then says "I am a worm" and we begin another picture/scene with different children jumping in to make a new picture/scene.

At the base this is a "yes, and" game. In the beginning just play it as written. As they get better at it, challenge the kids not to repeat too much. The third child will be tempted to just add whatever awesome idea they have already preloaded. Direct them to only add whatever fits with both the first and the second offer. Once you have the basics down, have them focus on different things for different effects. Make it all about the story they're creating, or all about the picture, or have them do it silently.

This is a great, all-purpose exercise that the kids love and you can use to strengthen many skills while continuing to hone the basics of accepting and adding.

I'm Cool and So Are You

Warm-up
Bonding

The children sit in a circle. There are enough chairs for all the kids minus one. One child stands in the middle and says "I'm cool and so are you if…" and says something that's true for them. If that statement is true for any other child then the other children get up and switch to another chair in the circle. Whomever is left without a chair is now the new truth-teller. You cannot go back to the chair you just left!

This is a great game for kids who are just getting to know each other.

Kitty Cat Careers

Warm Up

Have the kids in a standing circle. Start the chant with "Kitty Cat Careers," clap twice then repeat "Kitty Cat Careers." Then a kid will take the center of the circle and start miming some job or occupation AS A CAT—so it might be a cat train conductor or a cat doctor. They are allowed to meow, but not talk. The other kids call out guesses until one is correct. The kid in the middle will then face the kid who was correct (it's fun if they are a bit too close and loud) and the whole group will chant: "Kitty Cat Careers," clap twice, repeat "Kitty Cat Careers." The guesser usually goes next, but you can, of course, send it to a kid who hasn't gotten to go yet. The kids usually want to play this game for quite a while. As long as they are still being loud and making fun guesses, it continues to have value.

This game is great for working on space work and for getting in tune with each other.

Mirroring

Exercise

Have the children in pairs facing each other. One child will begin to move slowly, while the other child will try to follow along as if they're the mirror. Go on for a little while and then have the children switch. You'll need to coach them to go slowly and remind them that they're trying to be so smooth that I can't tell who is leading and who is following. After you call the switching for a while, tell them that they can switch without calling it—the following child will just start to move and then the other child will have to follow. If that sounds confusing, it's good—see if they can get to the place where they don't really know who is leading and who is following! Another variation is to ask them to do the opposite of whatever the leading child is doing.

This is a great exercise for children who need help with sharing control.

Moving Bodies

Performance Game

Two children are on stage and will stay in a neutral, frozen position. Two audience volunteers or other children in the class will *gently* put these children into whatever position they like by moving their arms and legs. The performing children will start the scene by talking, but they cannot move unless the other children move them.

This is a fun game for sharing control, because the talkers can say something that will push the movers to move them in a specific way. But the movers can also move them and then the talkers have to justify why they're now doing what they're doing.

Musical Eye Contact

Performance Game

Start with two children on stage. When music is playing, they must make intense eye contact. When the music stops, they must NOT make any eye contact at all. You can use this game to make things more dramatic or deeper, or you can just use it as a way to create a silly scene. Teens especially love this.

This game is particularly good for kids who are not really engaging with the other kids in the scene.

New Choice

Performance Game

Two children will begin a scene on stage. You will hold a bell (or just say "Ding.") From time to time you will ring the bell and the child who is speaking immediately has to say something different from the last thing they said. You keep ringing the bell until you're satisfied. Do this for both children, increasing the pace as the scene continues. It's particularly fun to do this for lists of things. For example:

"My favorite ice cream is vanilla."
Ding
"Strawberry."
Ding
"Cow."
Silence
"Cow because that's where ice cream comes from!"

This is a great game for children who make questionable choices as you can direct them to make more appropriate choices.

Norwegian Chairs

Warm-up
Bonding

To start you will need a fair amount of space and one chair in play for each child—it will help to have any other chairs turned or stacked so the kids know they're not in play. Have the children move the chairs into a random pattern and then each child should sit in a chair. Call one child up, leaving their chair empty. This child is the walker. They will start several feet away from any of the chairs and walk SLOWLY—tell them to use a funny walk to slow them down—towards the empty chair. The walker's goal is to sit in any open chair. The rest of the kids work together to keep that from happening. The only way they can keep the walker from sitting in a chair is if they themselves are sitting in that chair. You'll have to coach the kids not to hover over two chairs, or push the walker out of the way, or do anything to disable the chairs. Also, if you get up from a chair you have to go sit in a different chair, you can't just sit back in the same chair, unless you have sat in another chair first.

This game goes very fast—it usually takes less than a minute for the walker to sit down in a chair. Once they have sat, pick another child to be the new walker. As they do this, start pointing out that they can communicate with each other. The more they work together the longer they will keep the walker from sitting. However, I've never seen this go longer than a minute or two.

This is a great game for children who push for their way too much as it forces them to work with the group and any lack of trust will end with the walker finding a seat.

One Frog

Warm-up

Have the kids start in a circle. The first child says "One frog." The next child says "Two eyes." The next child says "Four legs." The next child says "Kerplunk into the pond." The next child says "Two Frogs." Then "Four Eyes." Then "Eight Legs." The next child says "Kerplunk." The next child says "Kerplunk into the pond." And this keeps increasing with the number of frogs. It's important to remember that one child at a time says the "Kerplunk." When you have reached as many "Kerplunks" as frogs, the kid says "Kerplunk into the pond."

This is a great game for concentration and particularly good for calming down middle school kids. They can manage the math, but it takes some intense focus and that helps them settle when they are too energetic.

One-Minute Monologue

Exercise

Have the kids stand in different parts of the room away from each other and facing a wall. The idea is to have them feel a bit of privacy. Then set a timer for 1 minute (or 30 seconds or 3 minutes, whatever you need). Have them talk in character or as themselves for the entire time. For shorter monologues you can give them a subject and just have them talk. For longer monologues it's helpful if you explain ways of sustaining monologues—for example, mention a memory, discuss some bit of philosophy, or make a metaphor to the current situation.

This is great for middle school and above. It helps them develop the capacity to fill out details of a scene.

Outlaw

Warm-up
Name Game

Have the children in a circle with you in the middle. Call out the name of a child. That child should duck and the children on each side should clap towards the ducking child. The one who ducks or claps last is either out or goes to the middle and calls the next name. If you play elimination style, once you get to only two children, have them stand back to back. They will walk away from each other until you give them the signal and then they will turn and clap. Because I am evil, I like to say numbers as they're walking and make the signal something like a multiple of three, so they have to do a little math.

This is a great game for kids who have a lot of energy and need to focus.

Pan Left/Pan Right

Performance Game

Have four children on stage, standing in a square about three feet apart from each other. The two children in front will be playing a scene, then when you say "Pan left" or "Pan right," the children must rotate to the left or right so that now you have one of the first children and a new child to the front. These children will play part of a different scene until you say

"Pan left" or "Pan right," and again they will rotate, a new child moving into position and starting a new scene with the two children who are at the front of the stage. When you introduce this, take suggestions for each pair of children as you rotate them through the different sides of the square by saying "Pan left" each time. This way the audience will understand what the game is.

As you play, look for good points to rotate. I like to let each pair establish their platform and then rotate them. After that look for any games that are developing and rotate to support those games. As always, go more quickly as the game goes on.

This is a great game for children who are just starting to understand the components of scenes.

Pass the Clap

Warm-up
Bonding

Have the children stand in a circle. Start out by clapping once, then the child next to you will clap once, and they'll keep going until you've gone all the way around the circle a few times. Then have the children pass the clap, but this time they will try to clap simultaneously with the child next to them. So Child A claps with Child B, then Child B claps with Child C, etc. Coach them to try to clap at the exact same time so it sounds like only one person clapping. Have them speed up and see if they can maintain the rhythm. Once they're able to do this well, up the challenge by having them clap across the circle rather than one after the other in the circle.

This is great as the first game before you introduce anything else.

People to People

Warm-up
Bonding

Before you start, let the kids know that if at any point they don't want to do something or something feels uncomfortable, physically or otherwise, they can always get out of it by saying "People to People." Have the kids in pairs. You call out two body parts, like "Elbow to shoulder." Then the pair has to figure out a way to match one person's elbow to the other person's shoulder. Then call out another two body parts. They will keep the first bodily connection—in this case elbow to shoulder—while also trying to touch the next two. After a round, let the kids start calling out the body parts. If they physically can't do it, or it makes them uncomfortable, or they just don't like it, someone calls out "People to people." At that point you drop all the touching and move to a new partner.

This game is great for teaching about working with people. It both emphasizes having boundaries and speaking out about them, but it also allows kids to touch in a way that's both silly and also very safe because they're controlling the amount and type of touch.

Please the Crown

Exercise

One child is seated in a chair and they're the king or queen. The other children are in a line. You should also have a space designated as a dungeon. The children come up one at a time and bow to the throne. You can work on stage picture here. The child offers the king or queen anything they like—rubies, a puppy, toilet paper. The king or queen either accepts the gift in which case the child is free to go, or doesn't accept the gift and sends the child to the dungeon. After all the children have given their gifts, you can announce "Jailbreak" and the children in the dungeon can break out of jail and run free. Then start with a new child on the throne.

This actually works for any age, but it's especially great for very young children.

Protest Signs

Warm-up

Have the children in a circle. They will be making up a four word protest chants one word at a time. The first child says the first word, the second says the second and so on until you have four words. Then everyone in the circle says the chant together twice. The next chant will start with the second child and go around to three more children and on and on until everyone has had the chance to start a chant. For example:

Child 1: "We"

Child 2: "Are"
Child 3: "Silly"
Child 4: "Bears"
Everyone: "We are silly bears. We are silly bears."

This is a great game for getting everyone working together.

Rock-Paper-Scissors Championship

Warm-up

Have the kids get into pairs and play rock, paper, scissors—just once. Whoever wins goes on to find another child to play with. The loser immediately becomes the cheerleader for the winner. When any child loses, all of their cheerleaders become cheerleaders for the new winner. You should end up with two children, each with massive cheering sections, playing each other. The final winner should be given lots of cheering.

This is a great game to end a class or to really raise the energy.

Sheet Game

Warm-up
Name Game

Divide the children into two groups. Have a sheet or some other cloth spread out vertically so that the children can't see who's on the other side of the sheet. One child comes forward on each side. When you drop the sheet, each child must say the name of the child on the other side of the sheet. Whichever child speaks last joins the other side.
This game is great for when children are having a hard time being wrong or letting go.

Slide Show

Performance Game

Have two kids set up on one side of the stage, pretending that they're talking about a recent trip. The other two to three kids will be in the larger part of the stage. The two narrators will say what kind of trip they're on and a little about it. Then they will show the first "Slide" by saying "One, two, three, click" so that the other kids have a chance to get into position (or you can turn the lights off for a count of three). When the lights come back up, or you say "Click," the kids on stage must freeze. The narrators will talk about this "picture" and what was happening while on vacation and how they felt about it. They will continue saying "Click" to change the picture from time to time so that the stage players can take a new position as a new "picture." It is great for putting kids into a role that will work best for them—either active or verbal.

This is a good game for sharing control.

Slo Mo Samurai

Performance Game

In this game have all the kids mill around the stage and then say "Freeze" when they seem nicely spaced. Each child is a warrior—from their elbows to their fingertips are poisoned swords. If they touch another child with this part of their arm, then the other child must immediately and dramatically die. The same part of the arm is also their shield. If they're touched on the forearm, the child is still safe. All of this happens in super super slow motion.

Children will have a really hard time losing in this game. Try to emphasize that the fun of the game is the dramatic death, and how Samurai were not supposed to value their own lives, but only wanted to do their duty. If two children are taking too long, battling it out, then I just yell out that they both die so that we can go on and the kids who did it correctly do not get punished. You will have to remind them to go slowly over and over. I will often just "kill" kids who can't slow down.

This is a great game for opening a show or ending a class.

Soap Opera

Performance Game

Have three children on stage. At all times one of the children must be staring intensely at the audience, another must be staring intensely at another person in the scene, and the third child must be splayed across some furniture or the wall. If any child changes, then all of them must change so that you always have one child doing each thing. Once they have this down, raise the stakes by having the audience make sure they're doing it. If there is not one child doing each thing, then the audience will say "Oooowwwwww" until the players adjust and get back to one child doing each of these things.

This is a great game for kids who need to move.

Sound Ball

Warm-up
Exercise

Have the children stand in a circle. You have an imaginary ball that you throw to one child while making a noise. That child will repeat the sound you gave to the best of their ability, and then will throw the ball to a new person while making a new sound. Let it go around a few times and then ask if anyone is pre-planning their sounds. If they are, give them some strategies for NOT pre-planning. Try to play this fast enough that the kids have to really just follow the thing before them rather than take time to "think" of the next sound. I will often lead them in moving their mouths and just making some silly sounds and letting them know all of those sounds are just fine. Don't try to make a cool sound, just make *a* sound.

This is a great way to get ready for accepting other people's offers.

Story Spine

Exercise

This exercise was developed by Ken Adams.
Have the children sit in a circle. You will tell a story together using these sentence starters:

"Once upon a time..."
"And every day…"
"Until one day…"
"And because of that…"
"And because of that…"
"And because of that…"
"Until finally…"
"And ever since that day…"

You'll need to coach the kids to not kill anyone until they get to the "until finally." Of course you can make it work, but it's a lot more difficult and it makes for really weird stories. You can also use this to tell the plot of popular movies or standard fairytale stories.

This is a great exercise for any kid who likes to write.

Taxi

Performance Game

Have four chairs set up to look like a front seat and back seat of a car. Have one child in the driver's seat, pretending to drive the taxi. If possible, they should still have a pretty strong character even though they're by themselves. After a few seconds a second child hails the cab with a different character. The first child takes on this new character, but they might retain their own concerns and ideas, but they'll copy the way the other child talks and moves. Then a third child joins them in the taxi and the other two take on this child's character. Finally a fourth arrives and they all take on that character. The taxi driver then stops to let the fourth child out, and the rest of the children go back to the third child's character. Then the third child gets out and they all go back to the second child's character. Continue this until you're left with only the original child driving the taxi.

This is a great game for developing characters.

Three-Headed Expert

Performance Game

Have three children sit on a bench or on three chairs next to each other. A fourth child will be the host. The three children will be playing one person who speaks one word at a time. The host will ask them questions or will take questions from the audience. The children will answer one word at a time. Coach the kids to accept what other kids have set up and not use their word to negate what another kid has said. You'll also need to let some kids know that they have to try to make sense, that trying to mess up the grammar or syntax will only make it confusing. At the same time however, the content doesn't have to be right or true at all—as long as the sentence makes grammatical sense, it's fine. The host will continue to ask questions until they feel like they have a good ending.

This is a great game for sharing control.

Touch Talk

Performance Game

The children will be doing a normal scene, but they can only talk if they're touching the other person. Pretty quickly they'll find the one place they feel comfortable touching and then just touch that over and over again. In this case you can coach them to find someplace else to touch. Obviously, they should steer clear of bathing suit areas. Middle schoolers have a very hard time touching each other, so maybe give them some ideas—like you can hold hands, touch their arm, push them with your foot, etc. But you can't say your line unless you're touching the other person.

This is great for kids who need to move more on stage or who need more connection.

Town Hall

Performance Game

Have one child on stage with something denoting a podium—this child is the mayor. The other children are scattered in the audience if possible, or at the front of the stage if that is not possible. The mayor announces some small problem they have in the town—not enough ice cream shops, or turtles blocking the road, or where to hold the holiday ball. The mayor calls on the children in the audience one at a time. They stand up as different townspeople, offering different perspectives on the problem. It's fun to push them to listen to the other characters so they can have a variety of perspectives on the issue.

This is a very fun game for ages 8 and up. It's great for character development and encouraging appropriate mischief.

Traffic Cop

Warm-up
Bonding

This is almost the same as *I'm Cool and So Are You*. The kids sit in a circle. There are enough chairs for all the kids minus one. One kid stands in the middle and says something that's true for them. If that's true for any other kid then that kid gets up and switches to another spot. Whoever is left without a chair is now the new person standing in the middle. You cannot go back to the chair you left! If the standing child ever just wants to shake things up, they can say "Traffic jam" and everyone will have to switch seats.

This is a great game for kids who are just getting to know each other.

Trust Falls

Warm-up
Bonding

The children stand in a tight circle with one child in the middle. The child in the middle closes their eyes and holds themselves stiff, and then falls. The children on the outside have their hands up and make sure the middle child doesn't fall to the ground, and push them back to the other side of the circle. Keep doing this as long as the child can stay straight and is having fun, then switch kids.

Younger children are not used to being relied on for anything so you'll have to coach them in this. It can be a powerful moment for the outside circle to realize that they can take care of someone else and the inside child to realize that others will be there for them.

This is a great game for a class that's running a little rough.

Typewriter

Performance Game

You'll have one child pretending to be at the typewriter. They're writing the story that will be played out. The other two to four children will be off to the side. As the writer tells the story, the other children come to the stage to play it out—they may speak and make offers and move, do whatever feels good to move the scene along. The author is also able to stop the action and add things or erase things and make something else happen. Kids in the 5-8-year-old range really love this game.

This is a fun game for sharing the weight of making a story happen.

Untie the Knot

Warm-up
Bonding

Have the children stand in a very tight circle. Have them reach into the middle with one hand and hold the hand of a child across the circle, not the children on either side of them. Then they all put the other hand in and grab another person, not the same person as before and not the children on either side of them. Once everyone is holding both hands, then have them try to untangle themselves. They'll have to communicate and be willing to go over and under arms to make it work. If it gets too frustrating then it's okay to end it early, but it's also okay to let this take some time.

This is a great exercise for kids who know each other a little bit but you want to help bond even further.

Waiter

Exercise

The point in this game is to give the child a really quick succession of things they have to talk about as if they're experts. One child is looking at a pretend menu and asking lots and lots of questions about what is on the menu. They should frequently interrupt the waiter to keep them from getting too comfortable.

This is a great game for kids who need help making decisions and not caring if they're "right."

Where Have My Fingers Been?

Exercise

Hold up two fingers and everyone chants, "Where have my fingers been? I say where have my fingers been? (Say what!) Where have my fingers been? I say where have my fingers been?" Then the first child points to another and tells them a location. The second child then makes their fingers do a little scene in that location. It's short and doesn't have to be good. For example:

First child: "A barn!"

Second Child: "Moo, I'm a cow." "Well, I'm a horse." "What does a horse say?" "Neigh!"

When they're done, they say, "And that's where my fingers have been."

This is a great game to play before getting into scene work. It takes the pressure off of them to make things up because it's just their fingers. A weird trick, but it works.

Woosh Bang Pow

Warm-up

Have the children in a circle. Send the "Woosh" sound in one direction, each child saying "Woosh" one after the other around the circle. When a child wants to reverse it they will say "Bang" and hold their arms in an X shape—at that point the other child will just say "Whoosh" back in the other direction and it will go around that way. Or they can send the energy across the circle by saying "Pow" and pointing at someone across from them. They cannot bang a pow. It should go very quickly and be pretty high energy. Once they have the rules down, encourage them to go faster and faster.

This is a great game for when children have a lot of energy and you want to get them more focused.

Word Association

Warm-up

Have the kids in a circle. The first kid starts by saying a word. The second kid thinks of a word that is related and says that word. This continues around the circle until you get back to the first child. Then all the kids together try to say each of the words that were said, starting with the last kid and working their way through everyone in order back to the first kid. You can go around the circle only once, or several times depending on how challenging it is for the kids.

This is a great game for concentration. It also helps with the kids who try to be too clever. The kids will quickly realize that it is better to be obvious.

Word at a Time Saying

Bonding

Have the kids in a circle. Together you will, one at a time, create a saying for the class. The first child starts with one word, then the child next in the circle says the next word, and so on until you have gone all the way around. You don't have to end exactly on the last child if it won't fit the saying. Once a saying is created, everyone lightly claps their hands and in unison says "yes, yes, yes, yes." You can do this once or several times depending on the needs of the class.

This is a great game for ending the class.

Word Restriction

Performance Game

Have three children on stage. For each child, you will assign them a number between 1 and 25. That child may only speak that number of words at a time. It's best if you let them count the words on their fingers. For example:

3 words: "I like pie."

7 words: "Me, too. Pie is my favorite food."

18 words: "Actually, pie is very good for you because it's berries and fruit in a wheat crust. So there."

Have them try to keep a scene going while keeping to their restrictions. This will keep them from thinking too much about the scene.

This is great for children who are very smart and try to think through scenes. It focuses their brain energy on the words and lets their imagination be free to actually just play the scene.

Yes, And Lines (Three Line Scene Start)

Exercise

Have the children in two lines on either side of the stage. On one side a child will come out and make an offer, then the child on the other side will say "Yes, and..." and will respond to the offer. Then the original child will say "Yes, and..." and will respond to the other child. You can end the scene there or continue as it feels good. When they're done, they will go to the back of the opposite lines. You can layer this with many other challenges. For example, by the end of the three lines they must have all of their platform information established—they have to establish where they are, they have to use names, etc.

This is a great game for working on "yes, and" so that children build off of each other.

Yes, And Parties, No Parties, Yes But Parties

Exercise

For the "Yes, And" party you will have the children sit in a circle. The first person says they will have a party and something about it: for example, "I'm going to have a swimming party." Then the next person adds something like "Yes, and there will be ducks in the pool." They keep adding around the circle until it ends up being a crazy party. Remember anything is possible including space aliens, giant water parks, and yes, even Justin Bieber. You'll have to watch kids who want to undo what the kids in front of them have established: for example, "Yes, and the ducks all fly away" is something that blocks the offer of the ducks. The idea is that once an idea is established, everything stays and other kids only add to it.

For the "No" party, the child says what kind of party they want to have and then the next child will say "No" and say what they want to do instead. This goes all the way around the circle. In the end, we ask if they were able to have a party. At this point the kids are usually frustrated and will say, "No, nothing happened!"

For the "Yes, But" party, the first child says what kind of party they want to have and then the next child says "Yes, but..." and then adds in their own stuff. Again, nothing much seems to happen in this.

You can use this to draw parallels to the improv scenes and games you're trying to do. Make sure you always end with the Yes, And party because it's always so much more fun and makes everyone feel successful.

This is a great exercise for kids who want to do everything themselves. It lets them see how much fun adding can be.

Yes, Let's

Exercise

Have the children in pairs. The first child will start the activity by saying "Let's…" and then say what they want to do: for example, "Let's dig for treasure." If the other child does want to do that then they will say "Yes, let's," and then they will pretend to do the activity until the second child feels satisfied. Then the second child will ask, "What comes next?" The first child will say the next thing they want to do: "Let's find a treasure chest full of spiders." If the second child wants to do that, they will say "Yes, let's" and they will pretend to do that. If they don't want to do that, then in a super high voice, with their eyebrows raised, they will say "Nope." Then the first child will say "What comes next?" and at that point the second child will say "Let's…" and will choose the activity. This goes back and forth with them sharing control over the scene.

This is a great exercise for kids who don't feel comfortable making decisions or worry that they're doing the "wrong" thing.

You

Warm-up

Have the children in a circle with one hand raised. The first child points with the raised hand to another child (effectively lowering their hand). That child points to another child, who points at another. This should continue, pointing only at children with their hands raised so that each child is only pointed at once and are only pointing at one person. This establishes your pattern. The first child then says "You" to the child they're pointing at, that child says "You" to the child they're pointing at, and it keeps going until they come back to the first child again. You continue this pattern over and over again until it becomes pretty easy. Then you establish a second pattern—instead of saying you, you use a category such as fruits or cars. Once this pattern is established and the children can do it pretty well, you try to do both patterns at the same time.

You continue layering patterns for as long as it seems to work. If you like, you can eventually add another challenge—for example, when a child says "You" they move across the circle to take the place of the child they're pointing at. That child should also point and move creating a moving and shifting mass of kids and making the other patterns layered on top much more difficult. I would not do this until the children are pretty good with doing at least three patterns.

This is a great exercise for kids who need to focus.

Zip Zap Zop

Warm-up

Have the children in a circle—one child says "Zip" and points to another child. That child will then point to another child and say "Zap." That child will then clap at another child and say "Zop." That child will then start over with "Zip." Whenever they make a mistake, all the children in the circle put their hands on each other's shoulders, lift one knee, and say "Ah-ooo-ga!" This should be loud and silly! The person who messed up then gets to start over. You'll need to encourage them to go faster and faster. Once they have mastered this version, feel free to add challenges such as doing zip, zip, zip, zap, zap, zap, zop, zop, zop. If they can do either one or three then it really makes it much more challenging.

This is a great game for getting children to focus.

Zombie Tag

Warm-up
Name Game

Have the children scattered around the room. One child plays a slow-moving zombie—it's more fun if they're making noises and are really scary. That child will decide on one person to go after. They will make eye contact and then go after them, ignoring all others. They can only follow the first person they choose. If they catch that child then the caught child is out and the "zombie" goes on to decide on another person to follow. The only way a child can keep a zombie from getting them out is by calling another child's name. At that point the child whose name was called becomes the zombie and goes after another child. The original zombie is returned to being normal again. While the zombie is chasing their prey, you'll need to coach both sides not to run since that can be dangerous and doesn't really teach the names as well as going slow does.

This is a great game for kids who have too much energy and need something to get it out

RESOURCES

These are great books for finding games:

The Play Book by William Hall
101 Improv Games for Children and Adults by Bob Dedore

These are great books for teaching about improv:

Directing Improv: Lead the Way by Getting Out of the Way by Asaf Ronen
Improv for Storytellers by Keith Johnstone
Improv: Improvisation and the Theatre by Keith Johnstone
Improvise: Scene From the Inside Out by Mick Napier
On Impulse: The Art of Making Improv Theater by Carol Hazenfield

These are great resources for working with kids on the Autism Spectrum:

Camp Yes And: Improv, Autism, and Equity.
https://yesand.indiana.edu/

"The Connect Improv Curriculum: Supporting Youth on the Autism Spectrum and Their Educator" by L. Alana and J. Ansaldo. In T. R. Dudeck and C. McClure (Eds.), *Applied Improvisation: Leading, Collaborating & Creating Beyond the Theatre.*

Developing Social Emotion Communication Skills through Adaptive Improv Theatre.
https://www.lacyalana.com/improv-for-autism-and-at-risk-youth

My website with a basic curriculum, videos on teaching and more:
www.JessicaArjet.com

For direct consulting contact:
Jessica Arjet - jessica@HideoutTheatre.com

ABOUT THE AUTHOR

Jessica Arjet is the Youth Programs Director and Co-Owner of the Hideout Theatre in Austin, Texas. In 2007, after years of teaching theater and improv in other venues, she created the youth programs at the Hideout Theatre. She frequently produces, directs, and acts in the award-winning "Hideout Kids," the Hideout Theater's regular Sunday children's show and traveling troupe. In addition to working with children, she also directs and acts in many improv shows for adults at the Hideout and she frequently travels to festivals to teach and perform. Some of her awards include: Austin Chronicle awards, Nickelodeon's Parents Pick award, B. Iden Payne nominations and Austin Critics Table awards. She enjoys writing, role playing games, and playing with her dog, Butterscotch.

ACKNOWLEDGMENTS

This book has been a labor of love and many many midwives helped it into being.

First of all, my sincere thanks goes to The Hideout Theatre—the entire community supports and encourages this work with children and for that I am so grateful.

To the children, parents, and teachers who make up the Youth Programs—this book is both for you and by you, for I could not have written it without your patience and enthusiasm in classes and beyond.

I would also like to thank the Hideout Management Team: Kareem Badr, Roy Janik, Andy Crouch, and Courtney Hopkin—many of the ideas in this book were honed in my discussions with you all and I am grateful for your insights.

I am also grateful to Asaf Ronen and Nadine Latief who comprised my writers' group and offered invaluable feedback and critique. The good company was also lovely.

Everyone needs a support system and I have so many people who have helped me—too many to name here. But I would feel remiss if I didn't call out certain people who have been my shelter in rocky weather: Laura Smith, Aspen Webster, Regina Soto, Lisa Jackson, Kacey Samiee, and Ryan Hill. Thank you all for the long talks, short texts, and everything in between. You all keep me sane!

Finally, to my kids Catherine and Henry Arjet who are amazingly supportive and helpful. I'm so proud of the people you have become!

And my partner, Andreas Fabis, who brings me delight and support in equal turns.

Made in USA - Kendallville, IN
1215081_9781950186266
12.17.2020 0726